American Poetry: A Very Short Introduction

VERY SHORT INTRODUCTIONS are for anyone wanting a stimulating and accessible way into a new subject. They are written by experts, and have been translated into more than 45 different languages.

The series began in 1995, and now covers a wide variety of topics in every discipline. The VSI library currently contains over 650 volumes—a Very Short Introduction to everything from Psychology and Philosophy of Science to American History and Relativity—and continues to grow in every subject area.

Very Short Introductions available now:

Available soon:

For more information visit our website

www.oup.com/vsi/

David Caplan

AMERICAN POETRY

A Very Short Introduction

OXFORD
UNIVERSITY PRESS

OXFORD

UNIVERSITY PRESS

Oxford University Press is a department of the University of Oxford.
It furthers the University's objective of excellence in research, scholarship,
and education by publishing worldwide. Oxford is a registered trade mark of
Oxford University Press in the UK and certain other countries.

Published in the United States of America by Oxford University Press
198 Madison Avenue, New York, NY 10016, United States of America.

© Oxford University Press 2022

All rights reserved. No part of this publication may be reproduced,
stored in a retrieval system, or transmitted, in any form or by any means,
without the prior permission in writing of Oxford University Press,
or as expressly permitted by law, by license, or under terms agreed with
the appropriate reproduction rights organization. Inquiries concerning
reproduction outside the scope of the above should be sent to the
Rights Department, Oxford University Press, at the address above.

You must not circulate this work in any other form
and you must impose this same condition on any acquirer.

Library of Congress Cataloging-in-Publication Data

Names: Caplan, David, 1969- author.
Title: American poetry : a very short introduction / David Caplan.
Description: [New York] : [Oxford University Press], [2022] |
Series: Very short introduction | Includes bibliographical references and index.
Identifiers: LCCN 2021029446 (print) | LCCN 2021029447 (ebook) |
ISBN 9780190640194 (paperback) | ISBN 9780190640224 (epub) |
ISBN 9780190640217 (ebook)
Subjects: LCSH: American poetry—History and criticism.
Classification: LCC PS303 .C37 2022 (print) | LCC PS303 (ebook) |
DDC 811.009—dc23
LC record available at https://lccn.loc.gov/2021029446
LC ebook record available at https://lccn.loc.gov/2021029447

1 3 5 7 9 8 6 4 2

Printed in Great Britain by
Ashford Colour Press Ltd., Gosport, Hants., on acid-free paper

Contents

List of illustrations

Acknowledgments

I would like to thank Kevin Clarke and Yehuda Halper. Both read the complete manuscript and offered very helpful comments. I also benefited from the insightful comments that Oxford University Press's anonymous readers offered on the manuscript. Ana Echevarria-Morales helped me in more ways than I can say. Nancy Toff and Brent Matheny gracefully guided this book to publication.

This book is dedicated in memory of my father, Edward Caplan זכרונו לברכה and in loving admiration for the selfless care my mother, Diana Caplan, devoted to him.

Charles Bernstein, "A Defence of Poetry," is reprinted with permission from Charles Bernstein. Roger Reeves, "Domestic Violence," is reprinted with permission from Roger Reeves.

Chapter 1

American poetry's two characteristics

Two characteristics mark American poetry. On the one hand,
several of its major figures promoted American poetry as
essentially different from any other nation's. Although the reasons
they offer vary, they typically claim that American experience
demands a different kind of expression. Such poets advocate for
novelty, for a break with what is perceived to be outmoded and
foreign. As Walt Whitman wrote, "Old forms, old poems, majestic
and proper in their own lands here in this land are exiles."
According to this view, America's newness requires a
correspondingly new literature. What is "majestic and proper"
elsewhere appears unimpressive and inappropriate here. As a
consequence, American authors bear the responsibility of
developing a literature suitable to their unique country, by
creating new forms and new kinds of poems. This emphasis on
uniqueness even informs the work of American poets reluctant to
commit to any national artistic endeavor. Inspired by it, they
too feel the need to create new forms and new kinds of poems.

On the other hand, American poetry hardly isolates itself from
international developments. Instead, it might be more rightly called
profoundly transnational. Its gaze extends beyond national borders
and its influences range widely. Just as individual authors move
between different countries, American poetry often welcomes
techniques, styles, and traditions originating from outside America.

"The American," observed T. S. Eliot, criticizing this characteristic, "shows his too quick susceptibility to foreign influence."

To understand American poetry, we must recognize both characteristics and their intimate, dynamic relationship. While, to a certain extent, all national literatures look both inward and outward, a particularly intense combination of the two characteristics inflects American poetry, influenced by its late historical emergence and rapid development. The two characteristics do not exist separately from each other. Rather, they work in a productive dialectic, inspiring both individual accomplishment and the broader field. Of the two, the first characteristic (American poetry's emphasis on its uniqueness) is often the easiest to overvalue and the second (its transnationalism) is the easiest to neglect. Especially when American poetry turns boisterous and assertive, the temptation arises to isolate it from other countries and their literary traditions. According to this line of reasoning, the more "American" a poem is, the better it is. At its worst, this standard translates cultural jingoism into literary terms. It reduces American poetry by enforcing a crude standard on a complex body of literature, overlooking the forces that energize it.

Instead, the two characteristics stimulate American poetry with overlapping, competing, and sustaining interests. Both drive the poetry. They animate the poet's choice of forms, meters, and language and the emphasis placed on originality, mastery of convention, or a combination of both. They add a certain intensity to the poetry and the debates it inspires.

These characteristics predate the establishment of the United States of America. Consider Anne Bradstreet, the first poet living in America to publish an original collection of their own work (though, tellingly, her collection, *The Tenth Muse Lately Sprung Up in America…*, *by a Gentlewoman in Those Parts*, was published in London). Bradstreet was born Anne Dudley in

American Poetry

2

Northampton, England, to a prominent Puritan family. Both her father and her husband served as governors of the Massachusetts Bay Colony. Tutored at home, Bradstreet learned Greek, Latin, French, and Hebrew. She also read the work of many canonical Anglo-European authors. At eighteen, she sailed to America with her husband and father. In 1650, *The Tenth Muse Lately Sprung Up in America…, by a Gentlewoman in Those Parts* was published after her brother-in-law brought it to a publishing house, without, Bradstreet claimed, her knowledge.

True to its title, the book locates the "tenth muse lately sprung up" in New England, reporting back from "those parts." The term "tenth muse" both connects Bradstreet to poets writing in England and distinguishes her from them. Like her English contemporaries, Bradstreet draws inspiration from ancient Greek and Latin sources, the muses of the Anglo-European literary tradition. She also represents a recent development: the "tenth muse" added to the classical nine. The nine muses date back to antiquity. Arising in a foreign landscape, the tenth is new.

In "A Dialogue between Old England and New; Concerning Their Present Troubles, Anno, 1642," Bradstreet seeks to define the contribution that a voice from the periphery might contribute. In the poem, America addresses England as England faces the imminent threat of a civil war. Noticing Old England's downtrodden state, New England solicitously asks, "What means this wailing tone, this mournful guise? / Ah, tell thy Daughter; she may sympathize." During the exchanges that follow, Old England admits the guilt she feels over her debased religious state, "my sins—the breach of sacred Laws." However, she never sufficiently answers her daughter's question, until New England presses her, "Pray, in plain terms, what is your present grief?" The almost blunt inquiry jolts Old England, inspiring one of the poem's most conversational moments:

> Well, to the matter, then. There's grown of late
> 'Twixt King and Peers a question of state:

American Poetry

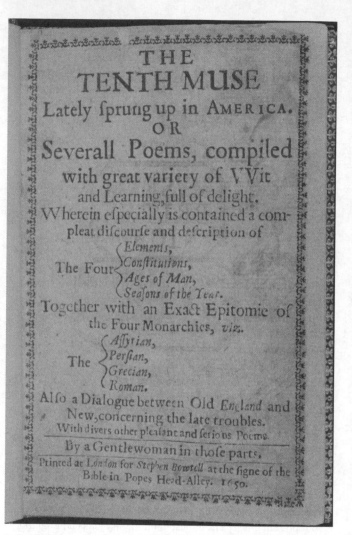

THE
TENTH MUSE
Lately ſprung up in AMERICA.
OR
Severall Poems, compiled
with great variety of VVit
and Learning, full of delight.
Wherein eſpecially is contained a com-
pleat diſcourſe and deſcription of
The Four
Elements,
Conſtitutions,
Ages of Man,
Seaſons of the Year.
Together with an Exact Epitomie of
the Four Monarchies, viz.
The
Aſſyrian,
Perſian,
Grecian,
Roman.
Alſo a Dialogue between Old England and
New, concerning the late troubles.
With divers other pleaſant and ſerious Poems.
By a Gentlewoman in thoſe parts.

Printed at London for Stephen Bowtell at the ſigne of the
Bible in Popes Head-Alley. 1650.

1. In 1650, Anne Bradstreet published the first collection of poems
written by a poet in America, presenting "the tenth muse" that had
"lately sprung up in America."

4

> Which is the chief, the law, or else the King?
> One saith, it's he; the other, no such thing.

"A Dialogue between Old England and New" employs many of the stylistic and rhetorical conventions of its day, placing the still-novel perspective of "New England" within the English literary tradition. When she personifies England as the mother and America as the daughter, she returns her readers to a familiar poetic technique, personification, and comparison. For instance, twelve years before, when sailing to America, seven Puritan leaders signed a document that faithfully called "the Church of England" "our dear Mother" from whom "we have received" "salvation" "in her bosom and sucked it from her breasts." The signers included Bradstreet's father. Recasting the personification, Bradstreet also employs a well-established verse form. The poem is composed in heroic couplets, the era's dominant verse form.

The poetic strategies Bradstreet employs cannot be separated from her theological and political concerns. They carry a particular charge. Most obviously, the poem exhibits the Puritan preference for "a plain style" distinguished (as William Bradford advocated) "with singular regard unto the simple truth in all things." When New England urges Old England to speak in "plain terms," she admonishes Old England to follow her own example and act in true Christian fashion.

This eloquence of this plain style should not be confused with an unlearned or artless expression. It need not lack passion (as also demonstrated by Bradstreet's most famous poem, "To My Dear and Loving Husband," a tender celebration of married love). In "A Dialogue between Old England and New," New England zealously urges Old England to wage a vengeful holy war against those whom she denounces as the church's enemies, both home and abroad. The poem gleefully details the violence that Old England should inflict on "the Church's foes"; "We hate *Rome's* Whore, with all her trumpery," she charges, urging, "Let Gaols be fill'd with th' remnant of that pack, / And sturdy *Tyburn* loaded till it crack." After sacking Rome "and all her vassals rout," England must not cease her bloody labors but "lay her [Turkey] waste," "and do to *Gog* as thou hast done to *Rome*." Like the poem's use of personification, its biblical and historical allusions employ a vocabulary familiar to Bradstreet's readers. They foreground the beliefs and (from a contemporary perspective) the hatreds that "Old England and New" share.

While New England presents herself as a dutiful daughter, the confidence and sophistication with which she addresses Old England remains the poem's most striking feature. New England speaks the poem's first and last words, the opening and closing lines. She asks the poem's best questions and gives the soundest advice. By comparison, the poem presents Old England as self-involved and, at times, petulant. Consumed by her troubles, her "fainting weak'ned body" and "wasting state," for instance, she never inquires about her daughter's well-being. Instead, she seems far less worldly than her daughter.

Scholars disagree about how to understand the relationship between Old England and New England that the poem depicts. One scholar reads the poem as a validation of the Puritan inhabitants of the New World's decision to remain in the New World; another sees it as evidence that "suggests she [Bradstreet] never really felt comfortable in America and that she often yearned for the land of her birth." The most rewarding way to understand the poem is to follow its invitation and to hear the "dialogue" it conducts between these attitudes, between self-validation and yearning. In the transatlantic dialogue, New England remains Old England's devoted daughter, but one who possesses her own perspective. New England deeply cares about Old England, closely following its political disputes and keeping many of its literary and religious traditions. However, New England also stands separate, not only geographically distanced but also confident in her maturity, bolstered by the sense that her mother needs her wisdom.

Nearly three hundred years later, Wallace Stevens returned to the question of how to understand America's relation to England, focusing, though, on the connection between the two countries' poetic traditions, not their religions and politics. To explore this issue, Stevens's "Autumn Refrain" contrasts two birds. First, the speaker remembers hearing grackles, a kind of blackbird:

> The skreak and skritter of evening gone
> And grackles gone and sorrows of the sun,
> The sorrows of sun, too, gone...

The inelegant grackle hardly resembles the nightingale, whose absence the poem laments:

> not a bird for me
> But the name of a bird and the name of a nameless air
> I have never—shall never hear.

Two facts inform the contrast that the poem establishes between the grackle and nightingale. First, the birds sound dramatically different. Emphasizing this point, Stevens's harsh, grating description of the grackles invokes the birds' harsh, grating song. "The skreak and skritter of evening gone" call to mind the guttural "squeaks, whistles, and croaks" these birds make, which ornithologists describe as "sounding like a rusty gate." In contrast, the famously mellifluous nightingale inspires much more pleasant associations. "Messenger of spring, nightingale with enticing song," Sappho called it.

Inspired by this "enticing song," authors have long represented the nightingale as a figure for the poet. This history extends through canonical Anglo-European literature, starting with Greco-Roman authors such as Homer, Ovid, and Sappho and continuing in the English Renaissance with John Milton and Edmund Spenser, among others. The association of the poet as a nightingale, however, achieved its greatest expression in English Romantic poetry, most prominently with John Keats's "Ode to a Nightingale" and Percy Bysshe Shelley's "A Defence of Poetry," where Shelley asserts, "A poet is a nightingale who sits in darkness and sings to cheer its own solitude with sweet sounds."

Second, Stevens's poem exploits a geographic fact about the birds: the nightingale is native to western Europe and northern Africa, while the grackles are found throughout North America. The birds' natural habitats do not overlap. When the speaker of "Autumn Refrain" acknowledges "I have never—shall never hear" the nightingale, he speaks, like Stevens, as an American in America, who has never traveled to Europe and never will.

In "Autumn Refrain," Stevens combines literary history and national geography. The nightingale represents the unlived life, the Anglo-European poetry the speaker experiences only secondhand. He laments that he will never directly encounter the nightingale's song or the literary history it represents. The grackle does not offer comparable pleasures or status. Even when not compared to the sweetly musical nightingale, the noisy, guttural grackle hardly presents an attractive figure for the American poet.

Nearly three hundred years of cultural, religious, and literary history separate Bradstreet's and Stevens's poems. Stevens does not share Bradstreet's Puritan faith. A modernist, he self-consciously wrote during what he called the twentieth century's "age of disbelief." "To see the gods dispelled in mid-air," he declared, "and dissolve like clouds is one of the great human experiences...It is simply that they came to nothing." Instead of a plain style, Stevens celebrated what he called "the essential gaudiness of poetry," a delight in language's flamboyant, nonrational properties. Bradstreet would never write lines as fanciful as Stevens's command to a fellow poet seated at a piano: "Play the present, its hoo-hoo-hoo, / Its shoo-shoo-shoo, its ric-a-nic." For Stevens, though, a poem's sounds do not exist merely to reinforce the expressed meaning, to echo the sense. Instead, they perform what Stevens saw as poetry's noble function: "It is a violence from within that protects us from a violence without. It is the imagination pressing back against the pressure of reality. It seems, in the last analysis, to have something to do with our self-preservation; and that, no doubt, is why the expression of it, the sound of its words, helps us to live our lives." Poetry exerts a counterforce called "imagination"; it resists the violent impositions of "reality" upon it. Whether fanciful or somber, the sound "helps us to live our lives."

Lamenting his geographic and literary estrangement, Stevens employs a more restrained language in "Autumn Refrain." The nightingale, "not a bird for me," remains outside the American landscape and, by extension, American literature. Without the nightingale's inspiration, the American poet cannot follow Keats or Shelley. The riddling, desolate poem, though, also offers a faint hope: "something resides, / Some skreaking and skrittering residuum." "Autumn Refrain" describes a moment of stillness that follows the grackle's noisy song: "And the stillness is in the key, all of it is, / The stillness is all in the key of that desolate sound." The silence bears a trace of the nightingale's unheard song, a "residuum" the speaker experiences only secondhand in the imagination, as well as a trace of the grackle's guttural sound. Both the remembered and the imagined birdsong intensify the absence the speaker encounters.

By implication, Stevens suggests the dilemma he believes the modern American poet faces. "Autumn Refrain" presents English and American poetry as both separate and intimately connected. Distanced by time and geography, the American poet cannot directly experience the nightingale and the Anglo-European traditions it represents. In this sense, the poem distinguishes American and English poetry. Like the grackle and nightingale, they belong to different climates and sound quite different. Neither would be confused for the other. The speaker, though,

9

experiences the "residuum" of both. The nightingale's absence haunts him: it contributes to the stillness that he experiences no less than the grackle's harsh song. Just as the speaker cannot hear the grackle, the native American bird, without thinking of the foreign nightingale, the American poet remains consumed with the English literary tradition his work follows but does not belong to. Its palpable absence deepens the "desolate sound" the speaker hears and the poem makes.

Bradstreet and Stevens explore American poetry's connection with its earliest historical influence, England. American poetry's interest in other countries and their literature extends far beyond that one example. In many cases, personal and familial histories inspire American poets to write in an international context. Their American poetry hardly stands removed from other literatures and culture. Instead, their work migrates widely across national borders, feeding on new landscapes, inspirations, and questions.

According to his account, Langston Hughes wrote his most famous poem, "The Negro Speaks of Rivers," as the train he took from St. Louis to Mexico to visit his father passed over the Mississippi. At the time, Hughes was seventeen years old. "All day on the train I had been thinking about my father and his strange dislike of his own people," Hughes remembered. "I didn't understand it, because I was a Negro, and I like Negroes very much." In "The Negro Speaks of Rivers," Hughes replaces his father's racial self-hatred with his own racial self-identification, rooted in American geography and history but also extending beyond them:

> I've known rivers:
> I've known rivers ancient as the world and older than the flow of
>   human blood in human veins.
> My soul has grown deep like the rivers.
> I bathed in the Euphrates when dawns were young.

I built my hut near the Congo and it lulled me to sleep.

I looked upon the Nile and raised the pyramids above it.

I heard the singing of the Mississippi when Abe Lincoln went
      down to New Orleans, and I've seen its muddy bosom turn all
      golden in the sunset.

I've known rivers:

Ancient, dusky rivers.

My soul has grown deep like the rivers.

The poem presents ancestral memory, not autobiographical disclosure. The experience it depicts exceeds that of any one life. Traveling across continents and historical eras, it describes three rivers rather succinctly (in thirteen words or fewer): the Euphrates, Congo, and the Nile. The references to the Euphrates and the Nile evoke events that took place at different epochs in antiquity. They respectively mention "when dawns were young" and the building of the pyramids. The reference to the "Congo" more forthrightly straddles contemporary and earlier history. A scholar has called the Congo "a pastoral, nourishing, *maternal* setting" for the poem, suggested by the speaker's memory: "it lulled me to sleep." The Congo also carries a harsher association: King Leopold's violent exploitation of its population and resources. (The following line's mention of the building of the pyramids reinforces the reference to slavery.) When "The Negro Speaks of Rivers" appeared in Hughes's debut collection, *The Weary Blues*, a poem close to it, "Proem," more directly mentioned this oppression, declaring, "The Belgians cut off my hands in the Congo." Taken together, the three rivers suggest the grandeur and suffering of Black history. They evoke the African roots of civilization and slavery's painful legacy into the twentieth century.

The fourth river, the Mississippi, differs from the first three; it serves as the great mythic river of American culture and literature. T. S. Eliot noted the river's stature in Twain's novels: "the

11

Mississippi of Mark Twain is not only the river known to those who voyage on it or live beside it, but the universal river of human-life—more universal, indeed, than the Congo of Joseph Conrad. For Twain's readers anywhere, the Mississippi is the river."

Hughes's description depicts a more specific event: Abraham Lincoln's journeys on the Mississippi in 1828 and 1831, which formed the future president's "first real encounter with slavery." "The impact of these visits on Lincoln's views of slavery, however, must remain a matter of speculation," the historian Eric Foner concludes. Hughes more confidently described these trips as a turning point in American history:

> I looked out the window of the Pullman at the great muddy river flowing down toward the heart of the South, and I began to think what that river, the old Mississippi, had meant to Negroes in the past—how to be sold down the river was the worst fate that could overtake a slave in times of bondage. Then I remembered reading how Abraham Lincoln had made a trip down the Mississippi on a raft to New Orleans, and how he had seen slavery at its worst, and had decided within himself that it should be removed from American life.

The Mississippi forms the poem's inspiration and primary scene. It also receives the most detailed description, including the poem's only name, "Abe Lincoln," and the most developed image: "I've seen its muddy bosom turn all golden in the sunset."

"The Negro Speaks of Rivers" returns to what Hughes calls a pivotal moment in "American life." Like Hughes's train journey from America to Mexico, it crosses national borders, yet remains distinctively American. Its cadences draw from Walt Whitman and Carl Sandburg, two of Hughes's early influences. The poem also presents a longer, historical, mystical knowledge. It offers a racial wisdom forged by ancestral memory. The repeated line, "My soul has grown deep like the rivers," insists on this point: that the poem draws from the soul's ancient knowledge, accumulated over great expanses of time and distance, not limited by them.

Hughes traveled widely, both within America and abroad. In 1932 and 1933, he visited the Soviet Union with twenty-two other African American artists and intellectuals hired to make a film about African American life in the South. The film was never made, but Hughes's time in the Soviet Union inspired him. He wrote a number of poems that expressed what one of his biographers calls Hughes's "steady move to the left." "Good Morning Revolution," a parody of Sandburg's "Good Morning, America," greets the revolution, not Hughes's home country, "You are the very best friend / I ever had." (Not surprisingly, *The Saturday Evening Post* rejected the poem after Hughes puzzlingly submitted it.) "Goodbye Christ" is even more explosive. "Make way for a new guy with no religion at all," it announces: "A real guy named / Marx Communist Lenin Peasant Stalin Worker ME." Written in the Soviet Union, the poem calls for an international workers' movement with distinctly American touches. Hughes bitingly decries the "Rockefeller Church" and "Saint Aimee McPherson," a reference to Aimee Semple McPherson, a prominent American evangelical embroiled in a number of sexual and financial scandals, including a kidnapping that many believed was faked.

Hughes paid a price for his incendiary poem. McPherson's followers, accompanied by "a sound-truck blaring a recording of 'God Bless America,'" picketed a reading Hughes was scheduled to give, leading to him to withdraw from it. More damagingly, a number of anti-Communists used the poem to attack Hughes. "Hughes, you will recall, is the Negro Communist poet famous for the Communistic, atheistic poem, 'Goodbye Christ,'" J. Edgar Hoover's aide advised him in a memo.

Subpoenaed to appear before the Senate Permanent Subcommittee on Investigations, Hughes faced a number of

2. **Langston Hughes testifies before Senate Permanent Subcommittee on Investigations about his explosive poem "Goodbye Christ" in 1953.**

pointed questions about "Goodbye Christ." Hughes defended himself in several different ways. He called "Goodbye Christ" "an ironical and satirical poem." When pressed about particular passages, he demurred "that poetry may mean many things to many people." Switching tactics, he described "Goodbye Christ" as a dramatic monologue, a poem written in the voice of a speaker notably different than that of the author:

> I have explained the poem for twenty-two years, I believe, or twenty years, in my writings in the press, and my talks as being a satirical poem, which I think a great pity that anyone should think of the Christian religion in those terms, and great pity that sometimes we have permitted the church to be disgraced by people who have used it as a racketeering force. That poem is merely the story of racketeering in religion and misuse of religion as might have been seen through the eyes at that time of a young Soviet citizen who felt

> very cocky and said to the whole world, "See what people do for
> religion. We don't do that." I write a character piece sometimes as in
> a play. I sometimes have in a play a villain. I do not believe in that
> villain myself.

Hughes's cagey defense does not fully renounce the poem. Rather, it shifts responsibility for the ideas it expresses and limits its scope to an attack on religious hypocrisy, not a call for worldwide political revolution. The poem, though, bears no markers of a Soviet speaker, let alone "a young Soviet citizen who felt very cocky." Instead, American slang and references abound. Grilled by the subcommittee's members and its chief counsel, Roy Cohn, Hughes needed to invent a villain, one who speaks without the author's endorsement. Hughes deflected blame for the radical socialist atheism by recasting it as a sign of Soviet arrogance. He did not deny that the poem criticizes "racketeering in religion and misuse of religion." However, Hughes also added, "I do not believe in that villain myself."

The poem, though, does echo points that Soviet propaganda often raised. As a scholar notes, "Goodbye Christ" echoes "Soviet anti-religious propaganda and campaigns for the 'new Soviet man,'" the calls for Marxism to replace Christianity and create a new revolutionary personality: "Marx Communist Lenin Peasant Stalin Worker ME." Hughes's testimony strips the poem of its revolutionary charge. This strategy shows the complex relation of American poetry to nationhood. The American author defends his poem by claiming it voices an imaginary Soviet citizen's ideas, not his, as if only a foreigner were allowed to criticize America in such biting terms.

Like Hughes, Elizabeth Bishop traveled widely, but haunting events early in her life did not allow her to develop a fixed sense of national identity. Bishop was born in Worcester, Massachusetts, in 1911. Because of tragic family circumstances—when she was young, her father died and her mother was committed to a series of psychiatric hospitals—she was raised by maternal and paternal grandparents in Nova Scotia and Massachusetts, respectively.

These childhood losses haunt some of Bishop's most famous poems. "*Time to plant tears*, says the almanac," "Sestina" notes. "One Art," a villanelle, catalogs a host of losses, great and small, that the speaker struggles to accept:

> The art of losing isn't hard to master;
> so many things seem filled with the intent
> to be lost that their loss is no disaster.

Both "Sestina" and "One Art" employ complicated verse forms to explore heartbreak. A sestina repeats its six end words in each of its six stanzas according to a proscribed pattern. A villanelle repeats the first stanza's first and third lines as the last line of subsequent stanzas. Adding to the formal challenge, the first and third lines of each stanza rhyme and the middle lines rhyme with each other.

Bishop's skilled use of the forms achieves contradictory effects. It asserts a sense of formal control, a mastery beyond the depicted grief. At the same time, the repeated elements intensify the sadness the poem expresses. The villanelle's refrain insists, "The art of losing isn't hard to master," and the sestina's end words repeat their despondent vocabulary as if condemned to them, "almanac," "child," "grandmother," "tears," "house," and "stove." In a particularly poignant acknowledgment, the speaker of "One Arts" admits, "I lost my mother's watch." Read autobiographically, the watch recalls how little time Bishop shared with her mother. The keepsake's loss severs a connection between the mother and the child; it adds a loss to the loss. The villanelle form works similarly, obsessively returning to and counting the sources of the speaker's grief.

Bishop's youthful movements between families and countries left her with a sense of not fully belonging to either place. Years later, she remembered how she felt when she and the other American schoolchildren "pledged allegiance to the flag and sang war songs." "In my Canadian schooling the year before, we had started every day with 'God Save the Queen' and 'The Maple Leaf Forever.' Now I felt like a traitor." In 1951, when traveling in Brazil, Bishop suffered a violent allergic reaction to a Brazilian cashew tree's fruit. After she recovered, she stayed in Brazil for eighteen years, supported by a modest trust fund, and published two poetry collections, including *Questions of Travel*, dedicated to Lota de Macedo Soares, the friend who nursed her back to health and subsequently become her great love. Bishop also published translations of several major Brazilian poets.

The title poem of *Questions of Travel* describes the overwhelmingly active, lush Brazilian landscape: "There are too many waterfalls here; the crowded streams / hurry too rapidly down to the sea." True to its title, "Questions of Travel" questions the traveler's restlessness that causes her to seek out new sights and sounds, the urge to see, for instance, "the tiniest green hummingbird in the world." Wondering whether it would have been better to "just stay at home," the poem adds a disorienting complication:

> Continent, city, country, society:
> the choice is never wide and never free.
> And here, or there...No. Should we have stayed at home,
> wherever that may be?

The poem's final line undermines what we think we know: what "home" means. After the previous line's almost commonplace question, "Should we have stayed at home," the terminal comma leads the reader to anticipate that the next line will introduce another idea, perhaps started with a new verb. Instead, the poem re-examines what it just said; it shows how hard it is to define the rather elusive place called "home, / wherever that may be."

The collection *Questions of Travel* is divided into two sections: "Brazil" and "Elsewhere." As this arrangement reminds us, American poetry's home is not always in America. For Elizabeth Bishop, America is "elsewhere," one of a number of places where her poems are set and where she derives inspiration. She writes American poetry "wherever that may be."

Chapter 2
American English as a poetic resource

In the title poem of her 2002 collection, *Sleeping with the Dictionary*, Harryette Mullen describes "taking the big dictionary to bed." A note pointedly names the dictionary the poet shares her bed with: the *American Heritage Dictionary*.

Aroused by American English, Mullen delights in its largeness. Her puns, innuendoes, and inflections express a carnal desire for the *American Heritage Dictionary*'s "unabridged bulk." "I've been licked all over by the English tongue," another poem suggestively declares.

Remarkably adaptable, contested, and diverse, American English is one of the country's great poetic resources. A poet such as Mullen partners with American English; she embraces it as a source of pleasure and inspiration. Seizing these possibilities, her poetry conveys an exuberant appreciation of the language's peculiarities, its quirks and openness to experimentation and cultural cross-fertilization.

The *American Heritage Dictionary* and the American English it documents allow Mullen to write a poetry both distinctively American and transnational. "It is significant to me," Mullen explains, "that my *American Heritage Dictionary* was compiled with the aid of a usage panel that included African American writers Langston Hughes and Arna Bontemps as well as feminist author Gloria Steinem." Mullen's use of the *American Heritage Dictionary* honors this history. It claims a specific heritage in which leading figures from African American literature and feminist thought serve as linguistic authorities, arbiters of correct usage.

Attentive to the racialized nature of language, Mullen explores American English's conflicted state. A political controversy inspired her prose poem, "Denigration." In an interview, Mullen recalled, "A white political staffer for the D.C. mayor was pressured to resign because he used the word 'niggardly'": "It has no etymological relationship to 'the n____ word' but it caused a commotion. So this poem was a commentary on the power of language, even when it's misheard or misapprehended. We're sometimes reacting to the sounds and not only the meanings of words."

"Denigration" circles America's most troubling word with cognates, actual and false: "Did we surprise our teachers who had niggling doubts about the picayune brains of small black children who reminded them of clean pickaninnies on a box of laundry soap?" Describing the poem's method, one scholar notes that Mullen offers "teasing variations on a racial slur," while another observes that Mullen "makes her readers hear a sonic racial terror." I think both are right: The poem's puns are both teasing and unnerving. They evoke language's ability to wound and the power it offers to rebut insults with cunning and style.

Mullen's poetry also combines American vernacular with European avant-garde artistic technique. Several poems in *Sleeping with the Dictionary* use a technique developed by a French-based literary movement, Oulipo. In N + 7, the poet replaces each of the source text's nouns with the seventh noun that follows it in the dictionary. Relying on linguistic coincidences and chance instead of traditional notions of inspiration, this method

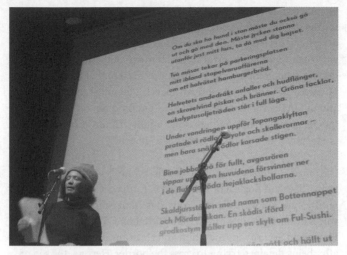

3. Harryette Mullen's work draws from international avant-garde techniques and American vernacular. Here, she shares her poetry with the audience at Stockholm's World Poetry Day in 2011.

introduces what Mullen calls "a playful strangeness," "aroused by myriad possibilities, we try out the most perverse positions in the practice of our nightly act, the penetration of the denotative body of the work." Mullen employs the N + 7 technique selectively in order to revise particular lines and phrases, not entire poems. This recasting of the *American Heritage Dictionary* bears the influence of the American usage panelists Hughes, Bontemps, and Steinem and the European members of the Oulipo, such as Raymond Queneau, Georges Perec, and Italo Calvino. By doing so, the poetry validates its assessment that the dictionary—and by extension, the American English it collects—is "a versatile partner, conversant and well-versed in the verbal art." Mullen claims and reinvents American English. She adds new uses and inflections to the language she discovers.

When poets explore American English's poetic usefulness, the diversity of their approaches and interests demonstrates the language's flexibility. "I am very fond of ordinary American speech for the poetic qualities I sometimes see in it," John Ashbery notes, describing his composition process as "picking things out of the air to use, and there's certainly no shortage of them." Ashbery describes his composition technique as akin to that of a collagist; he arranges "ordinary American speech," "handled in the right way and put in the right place." Ashbery's poetry often reveals the "poetic qualities" in language some might dismiss as lacking poetic potential: "ordinary American speech."

Of course, "ordinary American speech" is hardly an uncontested term. "Speak in English or the guard is gonna get us hermana / Pero qué hicimos but what did we do," writes Juan Felipe Herrera in the voices of two migrant women transported in a US Department of Homeland Security Immigration and Customs Enforcement bus after being detained trying to cross the border. Herrera, the son of migrant farmers from Mexico, writes bilingual lines split between English and Spanish. Their ordinary American speech does not limit itself to one language. Instead, English exists as a survival strategy and an imposition. Another poem offers a related point inspired by a different history. "Speak English / Forget the language of your / grandparents. It is dead," writes Linda LeGarde Grover, Anishinabbe, an enrolled member of the Bois Forte Band of Chippewa, recalling how the notorious American Indian boarding schools used English as a part of their efforts at forced assimilation. "Everything You Need to Know in Life You'll Learn in Boarding School" argues with the lessons it presents. A tension drives Grover's poem. The poem is written in English, the language forced on Native Americans. It protests, resists, and witnesses this imposition, what Joy Harjo calls "the civilizing genocidal process."

As these poems suggest, discussions of American English and its appropriateness for poetry often double as arguments about national identity. Any attempt to define "the American language" necessarily excludes countless alternatives rooted in different understandings of what defines America and its language. "Where do you draw the line between languages? between cultures? between disciplines? between peoples?" the postcolonial theorist Homi Bhabha asks in a different context. While some poets describe the language they employ as simply a fact of their surroundings, others more pointedly use a distinctively American English to explore these very questions, to signal or test a particular identity or identities. To put this idea in Bhabha's terms, some poets use American English to draw a line between languages, cultures, disciplines, and peoples, and others use it to question that distinction.

It is no coincidence that the historical periods in which American poetic culture most forcefully struggled with the issue of what, if anything, defined an American national literature coincided with the publications of dictionaries and studies devoted to the American usage: most prominently, the dictionaries Noah Webster published in the nineteenth century and H. L. Mencken's *The American Language*, first published in 1919. Some of these dictionaries inspired poets. Walt Whitman loved dictionaries; he wrote poems with Webster's definitions and not wholly reliable etymologies in mind. "The Real Dictionary," which he worked on but did not complete, aimed to "give all words that exist in use, the bad words as well as any."

First published in 1855 and expanded until months before Whitman's death in 1892, *Leaves of Grass* similarly bestows full respect on "bad words," ideas, even body parts. "The scent of these arm-pits is aroma finer than prayer," Whitman brags only a few lines after naming another area of the body seldom discussed in poetry, let alone praised: "I keep as delicate around the bowels as around the head and heart." Whitman's celebration of bowels and armpits did not escape his readers' notice. "In no work of the same size have we ever read so much that is disgusting and repulsive," charged a reviewer. "The author seems to exult in being as indecent, obscene, and profane as possible." Another reviewer called Whitman "one of the most indecent writers who ever raked out filth into sentences."

Two more appreciative responses are particularly notable. In 1842, Whitman attended a lecture by Ralph Waldo Emerson titled "The Poet" and heard Emerson declare the need for a national poet, calling America "a poem in our eyes" "yet unsung": "I look in vain for the poet whom I describe." "I was simmering, simmering, simmering; Emerson brought me to a boil," Whitman remembered. After Whitman sent him a copy of *Leaves of Grass*, Emerson responded with a warm letter of praise. Seizing the opportunity (Emerson was quite famous), Whitman excerpted a sentence, "I greet you at the beginning of a great career," printing it on the binding of the second edition, without Emerson's consent—and to his unhappy surprise.

Another reviewer recognized that Whitman had satisfied America's need for a national poet: "An American bard at last! One of the roughs, large, proud, affectionate, eating, drinking, and breeding, his costume manly and free, his face sunburnt and bearded, his posture strong and erect, his voice bringing hope and prophecy to the generous races of young and old. We shall cease shamming and be what we really are. We shall start an athletic and defiant literature. We realize now how it is, and what was most lacking. The interior American republic shall also be declared free and independent." The unsigned reviewer was Whitman; this self-review was one of three he published.

True to Whitman's self-promoting spirit, the figure of the poet claims center stage in *Leaves of Grass*; he is cast as both the representative democratic figure and its exemplar. The "American bard" may arrive late in literary history, but enjoys an immense advantage. "The Americans of all nations at any time upon the earth have probably the fullest poetical nature," Whitman crowed. "The United States themselves are essentially the greatest poem." The *Leaves of Grass* frontispiece bears a portrait of Whitman, bearded, casually dressed in a shirt open to the collar, his hand nonchalantly cocked on his hip, and his hat worn rakishly askew.

4. Ever the self-promoter, Whitman culled a private letter from Emerson to create literature's first blurb, stamped onto the spine of the leather binding of *Leaves of Grass*.

He looks defiantly American working class. Whitman purposefully presents himself as virile, going so far as to instruct the engraver to enlarge the depiction of his bulging crotch.

5. In the frontispiece to the 1855 edition of *Leaves of Grass*, Whitman presented his readers with a new image of the poet as "one of the roughs," attired in a workingman's clothes, with one hand in his pocket and the other casually resting on his hip.

The poetry continues the frontispiece's self-presentation. "I celebrate myself," the poem opens, "And what I assume you shall assume." Later the poet names himself:

> Walt Whitman, an American, one of the roughs, a kosmos,
> Disorderly, fleshy, sensual…eating, drinking, breeding,
> No sentimentalist…no stander above men or women or apart from
>   them…
> No more modest than immodest—

The poet introduces himself as "Walt," not by his more formal given name, "Walter," and by his nationality, "an American," and social class and demeanor, "one of the roughs." He is "no stander above" or "apart." Only a comma separates these three plain self-descriptions from a far grander one, "kosmos."

Whitman borrowed the Greek word from the Prussian naturalist Alexander von Humboldt's popular study, *Cosmos: A Sketch of a Physical Description of the Universe*. (The German edition used the spelling *Kosmos*.) Von Humbolt's notion of a well-ordered but diverse universe attracted Whitman; he also shared the naturalist's ambition "to depict in a single world the entire material universe." In a notebook, Whitman echoes this idea, defining *kosmos* as "a person who[se] scope of mind or whose range in particular science, includes all, the whole known universe." In *Leaves of Grass*, Whitman places himself in the center of that "whole known universe." Not limited to the more basic facts of a shared identity, the poet presents himself as mystically large and all encompassing. He invents an American English expansive enough to include French and Spanish malapropisms ("camerado" was a favorite) and other affectations. "Do I contradict myself?" he asks. "Very well then…I contradict myself; / I am large…I contain multitudes."

Developing a poetics to express this ethos, Whitman produced poetry both self-consciously egotistical and inclusive:

The camera and plate are prepared, the lady must sit for her
     daguerreotype,
The bride unrumples her white dress, the minutehand of the clock
     moves slowly,
The opium eater reclines with rigid head and just-opened lips,
The prostitute draggles her shawl, her bonnet bobs on her tipsy and
     pimpled neck,
The crowd laugh at her blackguard oaths, the men jeer and wink to
     each other,
(Miserable! I do not laugh at your oaths nor jeer you,)
The President holds a cabinet council, he is surrounded by the great
     secretaries.

Whitman crafted long, end-stopped, free-verse lines, meaning
they typically did not use consistently patterned rhyme or meter
and ended with punctuation. The sprawling lines extend across
the page and sometimes double and even triple back. Their
expanse allows Whitman to include a great many people and
details. In this passage, Whitman uses another favorite expansive
technique: the list. He catalogs a host of Americans from various
parts of society: "the lady," "the bride," "the opium eater," "the
prostitute," "the crowd," and "the President." Only the crowd is
disparaged, tellingly, because their members lack compassion and
demean the prostitute. (Whitman places a great value on
sympathy. To live without sympathy is a living death: "And
whoever walks a furlong without sympathy walks to his own
funeral, dressed in a shroud.")

The juxtaposition of the president and the prostitute is especially
striking. The poem treats them as equals. For Whitman, the
radical overturning of social hierarchy characterizes America at its
greatest. "The President is up there in the White House for you,"
he reminds the reader, "it is not you who are here for him."
Elsewhere in *Leaves of Grass*, he celebrates how the "common
people" and the president greet each other: "the President's taking
off his hat to them not they to him." Whitman's poetry repeats this

gesture. "The genius of the United States," he observed, is "almost most in the common people." To write as "one of the roughs" is to express America's genius.

It is easy—perhaps a little too easy—to contrast Whitman with Henry Wadsworth Longfellow, the most celebrated American poet of his generation. A member of two prominent New England families (the Wadsworths and the Longfellows), Longfellow taught foreign languages at Bowdoin and Harvard until a combination of royalties and family money allowed him to concentrate fully on his writing. He knew eleven languages, spoke five fluently, and traveled widely in Europe, spending several years abroad. He was the first American to translate Dante's *Divine Comedies* into English. In contrast to Whitman, who struggled to find a readership during his lifetime, Longfellow was an astonishingly popular, admired writer. While Whitman advocated for the establishment of a distinctively American literature, Longfellow objected when a correspondence invited him to take part in a magazine and a convention devoted to the cause. "A national literature is the expression of national character and thought," Longfellow responded, "and as our character and modes of thought do not differ essentially from those of England, our literature cannot."

Elaborating on this view, Longfellow's novel, *Kavanagh, A Tale*, presents a dialogue between the protagonist, a schoolteacher and aspiring novelist named Churchill, and a visitor, Hathaway, the founder of a magazine devoted to American literature. Churchill serves as Longfellow's mouthpiece. His ideas and language stay close to those Longfellow offers in the private letter. (The letter and Churchill's remarks even share some phrases.) When Hathaway tries to recruit Churchill to his cause of "a national literature," he explains: "We want a national drama in which scope enough shall be given to our gigantic ideas, and to the unparalleled activity and progress of our people.... We want a national literature altogether shaggy and unshorn, that shall shake the earth, like a herd of buffaloes thundering over the prairies!" The dialogue grows increasingly passionate as Hathaway presses Churchill, "Let us have our literature national. If it is not national, it is nothing." Churchill replies,

> "On the contrary, it may be a great deal. Nationality is a good thing to a certain extent, but universality is better. All that is best in the great poets of all countries is not what is national in them, but what is universal. Their roots are in their native soil; but their branches wave in the unpatriotic air, that speaks the same language unto all men, and their leaves shine with the illimitable light that pervades all lands. Let us throw all the windows open; let us admit the light and air on all sides; that we may look towards the four corners of the heavens, and not always in the same direction."
>
> "But you admit nationality to be a good thing?"
>
> "Yes, if not carried too far; still, I confess, it rather limits one's views of truth. I prefer what is natural. Mere nationality is often ridiculous. Every one smiles when he hears the Icelandic proverb, 'Iceland is the best land the sun shines upon.' Let us be natural, and we shall be national enough. Besides, our literature can be strictly national only so far as our character and modes of thought differ from those of other nations. Now, as we are very like the English,— are, in fact, English under a different sky,—I do not see how our literature can be very different from theirs. Westward from hand to hand we pass the lighted torch, but it was lighted at the old domestic fireside of England."
>
> "Then you think our literature is never to be anything but an imitation of the English?"
>
> "Not at all. It is not an imitation, but, as some one has said, a continuation."

"Nationality is a good thing to a certain extent, but universality is better": Longfellow's poetry favors a particular set of strategies to strike the right balance between these two imperatives. Like Whitman, Longfellow seizes on the opportunity to include distinctively American words taken from multiple sources and cultures. Stressing the reach of American English, Longfellow finds particularly appealing language that strikes him as attractively exotic.

For his narrative poem "The Song of Hiawatha," Longfellow drew from Henry Schoolcraft's studies of Native American culture, as well as what he called "other curious legends." The poem's opening credits Schoolcraft, referring to him by his Native American name:

> From the forests and the prairies,
> From the great lakes of the Northland,
> From the land of the Ojibways,
> From the land of the Dacotahs,
> From the mountains, moors, and fen-lands
> Where the heron, the Shuh-shuh-gah,
> Feeds among the reeds and rushes.
> I repeat them as I heard them
> From the lips of Nawadaha,
> The musician, the sweet singer.

In addition to Native American tribal and personal names, the poem incorporates Native American language. An author's note translates more than 140 Native American terms that the poem incorporates: in this passage "Shuh-shuh-gah," defined as "the blue heron." Similarly, in "The Jewish Cemetery at Newport" Longfellow pauses to note the names on the Jews' graves:

> The very names recorded here are strange,
>   Of foreign accent, and of different climes;
> Alvares and Rivera interchange
>   With Abraham and Jacob of old times.

"How strange it seems!" the poem's first line exclaims. The Jewish names attract the poet's attention for the same reason: their evocative strangeness. Instead of the expected biblical names,

31

"Abraham and Jacob," "Alvares and Rivera" recall an unforeseen ancestral history, lives born in a "foreign accent" and "different climes." The cemetery's Jews are Sephardic. They journeyed to America from Spain and Portugal (via Brazil).

Longfellow employs poetic form to organize the attractively strange American language, to make (in his terms) the "national" elements "universal." In this respect, poetic form achieves a very different effect than in Whitman's poems. Whitman's expansive free-verse lines advance the poem's national themes; they too seek to "give the sign of democracy." In contrast, Longfellow generally wrote metrical verse, poems that arranged accented and unaccented syllables into countable patterns. Longfellow's "The Song of Hiawatha" employs the meter of the Finnish epic "Kalevala." The trochaic hexameter (lines that offer six pairs of an accented syllable followed by an unaccented one) signals Longfellow's ambition to produce an American national epic akin to the European. "The Jewish Cemetery at Newport" is written in an elegiac stanza (four lines of alternatively rhyming iambic pentameter), the form, for example, of Thomas Gray's "Elegy Written in a Country Churchyard." The elegiac stanza highlights a shared solemnity. It associates the Jewish cemetery with more familiar churchyards and the ruminations they inspire. In both poems, Longfellow dignifies the "shaggy and unshorn" American material by framing it in European forms.

Literary history has been far kinder to Whitman than to Longfellow. The scholar Roy Harvey Pearce proclaimed that "all American poetry [since *Leaves of Grass*] is, in essence if not in substance, a series of arguments with Whitman," a claim that Ed Folsom fine-tuned, noting "how much American poetry has been in *substance* a record of that argument." Many poets have named Whitman as an inspiration not only for themselves but also for American poetry. June Jordan, for instance, called Whitman "the giant American 'literatus'": "As Shakespeare is to England, Dante

American Poetry

to Italy, Tolstoy to Russia, Goethe to Germany, Aghostino Neto to Angola, Pablo Neruda to Chile, Mao-Tse-Tung to China, and Ho Chi Minh to Vietnam, who is the great American writer, the distinctively American poet, the giant American 'literatus?' Undoubtedly, the answer will be *Walt Whitman*."

At least one of the poets on Jordan's list looked at Whitman similarly. Pablo Neruda told Jorge Luis Borges that "he thought of himself as being a minor South American Mr. Whitman." "I think of Whitman as one of the great gifts of America to the whole world," Borges added. Whitman's influence reached far beyond America's borders. "How often do I kiss your picture!," Fernando Pessoa proclaimed to him, while Federico García Lorca addressed Whitman as his "old friend." More recently, Luis Alberto Ambroggio's collection of what he calls "'Whitman-empowered' poems" makes the point more sweepingly. Its title declares, *Todos somos Whitman / We Are All Whitman*.

Far fewer poets have drawn inspiration from Longfellow since his death. (Robert Frost is a notable exception.) "Rarely has so respected a writer been so discredited by posterity," one of Longfellow's editors lamented. Subsequent generations shirked at Longfellow's appropriations and misappropriations; they noted the historical inaccuracies his poems offer. "The Song of Hiawatha" ends with a missionary conversion of the depicted Native Americans, while "The Jewish Cemetery at Newport" assigns Jews to the unredeemable past, since "the dead nations never rise again." Following Edgar Allan Poe's attacks on Longfellow's poetry, readers recoil from its didacticism, the neat Christian morality it expresses. Poets are more likely to avoid comparisons to Longfellow than to seek them. "When I'm told I have a large readership," the recent Nobel laureate Louise Glück reports, "I think, 'Oh great, I'm going to turn out to be Longfellow': someone easy to understand, easy to like, the kind of diluted experience available to many. And I don't want to be Longfellow."

However, if the passage of time has clarified the limits of Longfellow's vision, it is important to recognize the attitudes Longfellow contended with and sought to rebut. While Whitman opposed slavery's expansion, he did so because of concern for white laborers, not the slaves. As a journalist, Whitman steadfastly opposed abolition. Much earlier, Longfellow expressed a different commitment. When Edgar Allan Poe decried Longfellow's moralism, Poe expressed his outrage over the antislavery poems in Longfellow's 1842 collection, *Poems on Slavery*, which, Poe charged, "is intended for the especial use of those negrophilic old ladies of the north, who form so large a part of Mr. Longfellow's friends." Poe condemned Longfellow for a peculiar offense: "he certainly has no right" "by insinuating a falsehood in lieu of fact, charge his countrymen with barbarity." For Poe, the barbarity in question was not slavery. Rather, Poe objected to the "shameless medley of the grossest misrepresentation" because Longfellow depicted fugitive slaves hunted with bloodhounds, as in fact they were.

While Longfellow, Whitman, and their contemporaries in the nineteenth century grappled with the question of whether an American poetic tradition might be established, modern poets— that is, poets writing in the first decades of the twentieth century—contended with a changed political and artistic order. With characteristic brashness, Ezra Pound assessed the situation in 1929. "All the developments in English verse since 1910," Pound charged, "are due almost wholly to Americans. In fact, there is no longer any reason to call it English verse, and there is no present reason to think of England at all."

Pound denounced English verse as irrelevant while living in England's capital, London, a center of artistic activity and energy. An American expatriate in London, Paris, Rapallo, and Venice, Pound claimed what he called a "world citizenship." Reading Whitman abroad, Pound felt disgust for his native country and its poetic tradition. "He *is* America," Pound wrote of Whitman; "His crudity is an exceeding great stench, but it *is* America."

(Tempering his views of Whitman, if not America, Pound later declared, "I have detested you long enough... / Let there be commerce between us.") In Europe, Pound collaborated with many leading figures and agitated for the arts. It is hard to overstate his ubiquitous presence. He served as William Butler Yeats's private secretary, edited T. S. Eliot's "The Waste Land," and helped the careers of a host of authors including James Joyce, Robert Frost, William Carlos Williams, H.D., Ernest Hemingway, Ford Madox Ford, and Marianne Moore. He helped to found the influential literary movement, imagism, whose tenets he set:

1) Direct treatment of the "thing," whether subjective or objective.
2) To use absolutely no word that does not contribute to the presentation.
3) As regarding rhythm: to compose in sequence of the musical phrase, not in sequence of the metronome.

Imagism's emphasis on directness, economy, and formal invention transcended the movement, which quickly splintered into factions. Instead, these values inspired generations of poets, which surely was Pound's intent. Even the poets of subsequent generations who write in the English language's most enduring meter, iambic pentameter, must contend with Pound's boast: "To break the pentameter, that was the first heave."

In 1924, Pound moved to Italy and, during World War II, made a series of broadcasts that bitterly attacked the American government and American culture. Many of his statements were vitriolically anti-Semitic and racist. Some bordered on the incoherent, with language and logic so wild that some Italian officials wondered if Pound were speaking in code. As the war ended, Pound was arrested by advancing American troops, accused of treason, and placed in a metal cage in an army compound outside Pisa. After he was brought back to the States, much legal wrangling ensued until Pound was judged to be mentally incompetent to stand trial and was incarcerated in St. Elizabeth's Hospital, a psychiatric hospital.

While at Pisa, Pound wrote *The Pisan Cantos*, part of the hugely ambitious, ultimately uncompleted poem that increasingly consumed his poetic career. Part of the challenge Pound faced in *The Cantos* was to write a long poem that exhibited the prized literary quality of compression. *The Pisan Cantos* opens with an elegy for the Italian fascist leader Benito Mussolini. It laments the lost fascist dream, "the enormous tragedy of the dream in the peasant's bent shoulders." In places, the sequence presents a nightmarish version of Whitman's enthusiastic vision of American potential:

> "If you had a f…n' brain you'd be dangerous"
> remarks Romano Ramona
> to a by him designated c.s. in the scabies ward
> the army vocabulary contains almost 48 words

Pound presents American English as harshly primitive. The guards can do little with it except curse. Their severely limited language imposes another confinement and punishment on the prisoner, who is forced to listen to the "army vocabulary." Pound's elaborate syntax resists this crudeness. It pushes back against it with ironic gestures and qualifications, which turn Pound's jailors and the language they use into the butt of his joke: "to a by him designated c.s." and "the army vocabulary contains *almost* 48 words" (my italics).

The Pisan Cantos includes brief recollections of literary life abroad, shifting through layered memories. In the most beautiful section, "Canto LXXXI," Pound seeks to define what is essential and what is superfluous. "What thou lovest well remains," he insists:

> the rest is dross
> What thou lov'st well shall not be reft from thee
> What thou lov'st well is thy true heritage

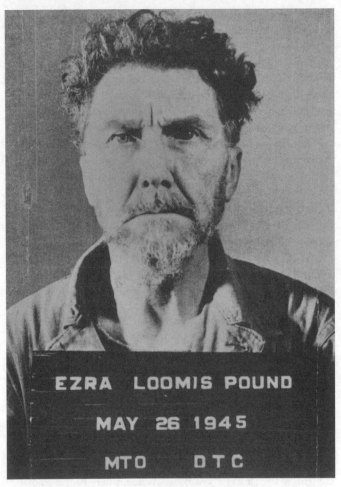

6. Arrested for his wartime broadcasts, Ezra Pound feared he might be hanged for treason. Supporters such as T. S. Eliot arranged for him to receive psychiatric treatment at St. Elizabeth's Hospital in Washington so that he would not face criminal prosecution.

The passage's archaic language pulls the speaker out of his immediate surroundings. It places him in a longer, grander, and nobler context. "Pull down thy vanity," the poem repeatedly implores, echoing Ecclesiastes, "How mean thy hates / Fostered in falsity." Pound does not specify whom he addresses. If he addresses himself, the poem might be read as an expression of regret for the pain and injuries his activities caused. In this reading, the poet might recognize his own mistakes and the "vanity" that inspired them. However, it is also possible to read the poem as primarily addressing the reader, urging him to set aside his deep-seated prejudices and misconceptions. If so, the beautifully rhythmic canto resembles other, less attractive sections of *The Pisan Cantos*; it offers another defense of Pound's wartime activities, another condemnation of the perceived injustice of his confinement. Brooding, Pound declares his innocence.

Trapped in his harsh confinement, Pound longed to return to places where he previously lived, cities of great beauty and culture, as in his longing for the sights of Venice: "Will I ever see the Giudecca again? / or the lights against it." Occasionally, he records a moment of surprising attractiveness. "As for the solidity of the white ox in the middle of all this," he notes,

> perhaps only Dr Williams (Bill Carlos)
> will understand its importance
> its benediction

"Dr Williams (Bill Carlos)" refers to Pound's friend and fellow poet, William Carlos Williams. Pound and Williams met as students at the University of Pennsylvania, where Pound studied romance languages and William studied medicine. For six decades, the two poets enjoyed an intense, complicated, contentious friendship. Early in their careers Pound used his contacts to help Williams publish his poetry. Eventually they exchanged more than five hundred letters. After Pound's release from St. Elizabeth's Hospital, he visited Williams at his home in

Rutherford, where Richard Avedon photographed the two old friends in their seventies, Pound shirtless, his hands resting on Williams's shoulders.

Significant differences, though, distinguished the poets and their careers. While Pound was a major figure in expatriate modernism, Williams worked as a pediatrician in Rutherford, New Jersey, and set his long poem, *Paterson*, in the nearby industrial city. Citing Whitman as a model, Williams advised American writers to explore what he called "the American idiom," "the language we speak in the United States," "characterized by certain differences from the language used among cultured Europeans." "We poets have to talk in a language which is not English. It is the American idiom." Williams's poem "This Is Just to Say" takes the form of an apology directed to the speaker's wife because he had eaten plums she had set aside. "Forgive me," he implores:

> they were delicious
> so sweet
> and so cold

The short, unpunctuated poem strikes a casual, colloquial tone. Its line breaks align with speech rhythms. This arrangement both makes the words sound as if someone were speaking them and intensifies the emotion of what is said. The poem expresses a delight in the pleasure that language gives. Forgetting his guilt, the speaker relives the taste and sensation of the plums. He lingers over the phrases, "so sweet / so cold" as his retelling prolongs his enjoyment.

Williams brought a particular sensitivity to American English, a perspective informed by his multilingual upbringing. Williams's mother was born in Puerto Rico; English was her third language (after Spanish and French). "I had the advantage of not speaking English," Williams remembered of his early childhood in a Spanish-speaking household; "That helped a lot." Pound's ancestors lived in America since the seventeenth century—and the difference between the two poets' family histories was not lost on Pound. "What the hell do you a bloomin' foreigner know about the place?" Pound wrote to Williams. "I," Pound noted, "have the virus, the bacillus of the land in my blood, for nearly three bleating centuries." (Elsewhere Pound called Williams "a mere dago-immigrant. Finest possible specimen of course.")

Referring to Williams in the *The Pisan Cantos*, Pound mixes personal and literary history. The image of "the white ox in the middle of all this" recalls Williams's poem, "The Red Wheelbarrow," which observes the importance of similarly colored animals, "white chickens":

> so much depends
> upon
> a red wheel
> barrow
> glazed with rain
> water
> beside the white
> chickens

Williams's description of a proletarian American scene keeps to imagist practice. He follows Pound's tenets, offering the "direct treatment of the 'thing,'" or, as Williams himself advised, "no ideas but in things." Williams constructs a poem of vivid particulars, not explication. The poem, for instance, never states what "depends / upon" the witnessed scene.

The qualities the poems share highlight the differences that separate them. A profound sense of isolation haunts Pound's echo of Williams's poem. Pound is incarcerated far from his friends and family, awaiting an uncertain future. (He feared he would be hanged for treason.) The observed "solidity" in the form of the ox offers a moment of relief, a "benediction." It confirms—at least to

Pound—his worldview and standing. Pound held a heroic view of the arts. He believed poets possess an occult knowledge of the world, shared only by a select few. Only an intimate like Williams, Pound declared, would understand the ox. "The Red Wheelbarrow" inspired Pound's aside, but Williams's poem expresses a very different idea. The exacting care it devotes to the depicted scene, the deliberate movements of its enjambed short lines, models an acquirable skill. The poem teaches the reader how to look at the world carefully and respectfully.

Williams's use of the American idiom resembles Whitman's in the sense that it necessitated experimentation with what he saw as a proper form for it. "Every time American strength goes into a mold modeled after the English," he explained, "it is wholly wasted." Robert Frost's poetry suggests the opposite. Frost sets American idiom—more specifically, the language of rural New England—in literary forms familiar to the English literary tradition. "Home Burial," a blank-verse narrative, employs unrhymed iambic pentameter to describe a marriage's painful dissolution. As the poem opens, the wife again stares out a window in their house. Not recognizing that she is brooding over their infant child's grave in the family plot, her husband impatiently demands, "What is it you see / From up there always—for I want to know":

> She let him look, sure that he wouldn't see,
> Blind creature; and awhile he didn't see.
> But at last he murmured, "Oh," and again, "Oh."
> "What is it—what?" she said.
> > "Just that I see."
> "You don't," she challenged. "Tell me what it is."

The poem not only describes a couple fighting; it also sounds like a couple fighting. The husband tries to buy time by repeating, "'Oh,' and again, 'Oh,'" but his wife confronts him with her own short, clipped, monosyllabic repetition—"What is it—what?"—a question almost as aggressive as her command that he display his ignorance, "'You don't,' she challenged. 'Tell me what it is.'"

The sharp exchange exploits what Frost called "the sound of sense," the ability of sound to convey tone and suggest meaning. In Frost's favorite illustration of this principle, a listener can gain a sense of a conversation conducted behind a closed door even though the listener cannot discern the actual words, only their sounds. "An ear and appetite for these sounds of sense is the first qualification of a writer," Frost maintained. "But if one is to be a poet he must learn to get cadences by skillfully breaking the sounds of sense with all their irregularity of accent across the regular beat of the meter." For Frost, the art of poetry organizes two different elements: language and meter. A poem combines the irregular "sounds of sense" with "the regular beat of the meter." Together, they achieve a powerful effect, an expressive coupling of the irregular and the regular, which Frost defined as essential to poetry, asserting, "Poetry plays the rhythms of dramatic speech on the *grid* of meter." Listen again to how the couple argues:

> She withdrew shrinking from beneath his arm
> That rested on the banister, and slid downstairs;
> And turned on him with such a daunting look,
> He said twice over before he knew himself:
> "Can't a man speak of his own child he's lost?"
> "Not you! Oh, where's my hat? Oh, I don't need it!
> I must get out of here. I must get air.
> I don't know rightly whether any man can."

The iambic pentameter lines follow "the regular beat of the meter," but not inflexibly. They employ well-established metrical substitutions. For example, an anapest (a metrical foot consisting of two unstressed syllables followed by a stressed syllable) follows the second line's mid-line comma, a familiar place for a metrical substitution, since the line pauses there. The fifth line in particular highlights Frost's method:

$$\text{u u / / u u / / u /}$$
"Can't a man speak of his own child he's lost?"

To use a contested term, the line might be said to employ two ionic feet: two groups of four syllables, whose first two syllables are unstressed and last two syllables are stressed. An iamb finishes the line. The line builds in emotion, culminating in the final phrase, "he's lost," the husband's bitter assertion that their child's death also caused him immense pain. He sounds angry and confused, and "the rhythms of dramatic speech," the line's sounds and tempo, express his anguish, all while keeping to the abstract conventions of meter, "the grid" of iambic pentameter.

Writing in an era when many leading poets explored free verse, Frost insisted on meter's enduring value. Espousing unfashionable views, at times he played the contrarian, quipping, "For my pleasure I had as soon write free verse as play tennis with the net down." Frost's own work remains far more interesting than his dismissals. Frost's first book, *A Boy's Will*, bore a title taken from a line borrowed from Longfellow, whose poetry Frost read "early and eagerly and he defended it well after it became unfashionable." Frost's metrical techniques recall earlier writers' preferences more than those of his contemporaries. Frost, though, often employs familiar meters and rhyme to explore ideas and situations as dark as any that his fellow modernists considered. He too felt modernity's encroaching pressures. "The highway dust is over all," another poem set far from any city observes, naming a quintessentially modernist task for the poet: "what to make of a diminished thing." In "Home Burial," the meter neither sooths nor alleviates the bitterness it expresses. The husband and wife share the iambic line, but the shared metrical pattern only emphasizes their profound estrangement.

Facilitating such effects, American English offers poets a remarkably adaptable resource. It allows them to explore a wide range of ambitions and disappointments. It helps them to express erotic discord and erotic inspiration, an egotistical exuberance or a focused attention to a few concisely presented details. They break the sounds of its sense across the regular beat of meter and cast American English into long, sprawling, free-verse lines or short lines consisting of no more than three words. They present American English as inspirational, equal to the challenges of nearly any meter, subject matter, or style.

Increasingly, though, a particular skepticism marks contemporary poetry. Many contemporary poets lack Mullen's playfulness toward American English. Instead, they share a tendency to present American English as deeply implicated in America's injustice and state-sanctioned aggression. Rae Armantrout explains that she and other poets associated with the avant-garde movement, language poetry, "came of age so to speak, poetically speaking anyway in the time of the Vietnam War and the time of Watergate and we became very much aware of language as spin." Decades later, Armantrout retains this sensitivity to "language as spin," as a means of social control. After quoting an unnamed gunman, "'I define terror,' / the shooter says // and types out the dictionary," she cryptically observes, "The government controls us / through grammar / and new currency." This tendency to interrogate American English marks poets beyond any one particular poetic movement. In a "Dictionary in the Dark," Naomi Shihab Nye similarly quotes American English to express her horrified distaste for its use: "A retired general said / 'the beautiful thing about it'/discussing war."

Emphasizing language as spin, such poems find military terminology particularly useful. Relentlessly, they expose language's brutality, its euphemisms and evasions. In her celebrated debut collection, *Look*, Solmaz Sharif builds poems from terms taken from the US Department of Defense's

Dictionary of Military and Associated Terms. Subtitled "an abridged list of operations," her "Perception Management" consists of over one hundred examples such as "RED BULL," "PITBULL," "BRUTUS," "HERMES," and "SLEDGEHAMMER." Without exception, contemporary American poets' politics are closer to Whitman's and Williams's than to Pound's, but lacking the animating faith in what Williams called "the very genius of the language," their poetry sometimes recalls *The Pisan Cantos*'s cantankerousness. At its least attractive, it tends to hector and scold, giving the impression that another demonstration of American English's inadequacy remains the contemporary moment's primary poetic task. Reading their work, I miss Mullen's playfulness, how she treats American English like a lover, intimately aware of its shortcomings, crafting language capable of both celebration and critique.

Chapter 3
Convention and idiosyncrasy

In 1772, eighteen colonial leaders gathered in Boston to perform a remarkable act of literary criticism. "The most respectable Characters in *Boston*," as they described themselves, included the governor and lieutenant governor of Massachusetts and several prominent ministers. The assembled men met to judge whether Phillis Wheatley, a slave woman living with her master and mistress in Boston, had written the poetry she claimed to have written.

Describing Phillis Wheatley's life, John Wheatley, her owner, also described some of the reasons why the tribunal was deemed to be necessary:

> PHILLIS was brought from *Africa* to *America*, in the Year 1761, between Seven and Eight Years of Age. Without any Assistance from School Education, and by only what she was taught in the Family, she, in sixteen Months Time from her Arrival, attained the English Language, to which she was an utter Stranger before, to such a Degree, as to read any, the most difficult Parts of the Sacred Writings, to the great Astonishment of all who heard her.
>
> As to her WRITING, her own Curiosity led her to it; and this she learnt in so short a Time, that in the Year 1765, she wrote a Letter to the Rev. Mr. OCCOM, the *Indian* Minister, while in *England*.

> She has a great Inclination to learn the Latin Tongue, and has
> made some Progress in it. This Relation is given by her Master who
> bought her, and with whom she now lives.

After an examination, the group declared in a joint statement, "WE whose Names are under-written, do assure the World, that the POEMS specified in the following Page, were (as we verily believe) written by PHILLIS, a young Negro Girl, who was but a few Years since, brought an uncultivated Barbarian from *Africa*, and has ever since been, and now is, under the Disadvantage of serving as a Slave in a Family in this Town. She has been examined by some of the best Judges, and is thought qualified to write them." This approbation appeared in the front of Wheatley's poetry collection, *Poems on Various Subjects, Religious and Moral*, published in 1773. Both it and John Wheatley's short biography of his slave preceded Wheatley's poems, underscoring the fact that she needed not only their approval to publish her work but also their authorization that the poems were actually hers.

The collection contains several poems that reflect on Wheatley's difficult life history. "On Being Brought from Africa to America" reflects on the author's journey to America:

> Twas mercy brought me from my *Pagan* land,
> Taught my benighted soul to understand
> That there's a God, that there's a *Saviour* too:
> Once I redemption neither sought nor knew.
> Some view our sable race with scornful eye,
> "Their colour is a diabolic die."
> Remember, *Christians*, *Negros*, black as *Cain*,
> May be refin'd, and join th' angelic train.

It is not hard to see why this poem has been called "the most reviled poem in African-American literature." Rooted in the author's personal experiences, the poem apparently celebrates

P O E M S

ON

VARIOUS SUBJECTS,

RELIGIOUS AND MORAL.

BY

PHILLIS WHEATLEY,

NEGRO SERVANT to Mr. JOHN WHEATLEY,
of BOSTON, in NEW ENGLAND.

LONDON:
Printed for A. BELL, Bookseller, Aldgate; and sold by
Messrs. COX and BERRY, King-Street, BOSTON.

MDCCLXXIII.

Published according to Act of Parliament, Septr 1773 by Arch.^d Bell.
Bookseller N.º 8 near the Saracens Head Aldgate.

7. **Phillis Wheatley's book identified the poet as "Negro Servant to Mr. John Wheatley."**

slavery as an agent of "mercy." It insists, "Twas mercy," not slavery, which "brought me from my *Pagan* land." The rest of the poem does not shy away from this startling claim. Instead, it neatly contrasts the "Pagan" and "Christian" lands of Africa and America. In places, the poem nearly reproduces the very language and logic others used against Wheatley. When she describes "my benighted soul" that needed "to understand / That there's a God, that there's a *Saviour* too," her self-portrait matches the tribunal's characterization of her as "an uncultivated Barbarian from *Africa*." Even when the poem criticizes prejudice, it does not condemn its most obvious manifestation, slavery. In fact, the poem shows how a more enlightened racial view might support slavery. When the closing lines contest the view that "Negroes" are incapable of salvation, the defense of the Africans' spiritual potential might be understood to undercut an antislavery argument. If slavery brings lost souls to redemption, Christians bear an obligation to use this institution to let others "be refin'd, and join th' angelic train."

Poems on Various Subjects, Religious and Moral also contains a
longer, more complex rumination on American slavery and
freedom, a verse epistle addressed to William, Earl of Dartmouth,
England's secretary of state for the colonies. The poem rousingly
encourages the English colonial representative to stand for the
"common good":

> Should you, my lord, while you peruse my song,
> Wonder from whence my love of Freedom sprung,
> Whence flow these wishes for the common good,
> By feeling hearts alone best understood,
> I, young in life, by seeming cruel fate
> Was snatch'd from Afric's fancy'd happy seat:
> What pangs excruciating must molest,
> What sorrows labour in my parent's breast?
> Steel'd was that soul and by no misery mov'd
> That from a father seiz'd his babe belov'd:
> Such, such my case. And can I then but pray
> Others may never feel tyrannic sway?

Wheatley again invokes her own personal experience as a slave, but
does so in order to advance a different notion of freedom and tyranny.
The passage describing her kidnapping starts and ends with
Wheatley emphasizing that she relates her own experience: "I, young
in life" and "Such, such my case." Her experience as a slave authorizes
Wheatley to address England's secretary of state as an expert. She
knows the necessity of freedom because she endured harsh tyranny.

Wheatley's argument for American independence doubles as an
argument for emancipation. She portrays America as a slave
bound in "iron chain." England might act as both slave master and
would-be liberator; she can free the American colonies from both
kinds of "wanton Tyranny." With greater delicacy, Wheatley
sidesteps the issue of America's culpability. The poem employs the
passive construction, "I . . . / Was snatch'd from Afric's fancy'd
happy seat," to avoid naming the guilty party.

Wheatley's neatly rhyming heroic couplets bear an extraordinary pressure. In the face of prevailing racial attitudes and debates about slavery, they sought to establish the author's status as a civilized human being. For this reason, contemporary assessments of Wheatley's poetry quickly moved beyond the issue of literary quality. To disparage Wheatley's poetry was to denigrate her humanity. Conversely, to accept her as a poet was to accept her as fully human. In a notorious appraisal, Thomas Jefferson pointed to Wheatley's poetry as evidence of what he saw as African American's racial inferiority: "Among the blacks is misery enough, God knows, but no poetry.... Religion indeed has produced a Phyllis Whately [*sic*]; but it could not produce a poet." In contrast, Voltaire praised Wheatley's poetry, arguing that the poetry demonstrated that "Negroes" were capable of "genius": "*Genius, which is rare everywhere, can be found in all parts* of the *earth.* Fontenelle was wrong to say that there would never be poets among Negroes: there is presently a Negro woman who writes very good English verse (She is named Phillis Wheatley and died in 1787...)."

To compose "very good English verse," Wheatley did not invent a new poetic form. Instead, she used her age's dominant structure. In the eighteenth century, a scholar of the period notes, "as the expected, almost obligatory mode for serious poetry, the couplet signaled ambition and seriousness." Heroic couplets' association with the classical past added to their allure. As the perceived English equivalent of the classical line, they joined contemporary poets with the canonical dead. Alexander Pope, the preeminent author of heroic couplets, used them for both his original verse and his translations of Homer.

The heroic couplet's status partly explains why it attracted Wheatley; she aimed to express the proper "ambition and seriousness." To achieve this effect, Wheatley did not disguise her influences. She celebrated them. In "An Essay on Criticism," Pope famously slowed the verse line to align sound and sense:

"The line too labours, and the words move slow." Wheatley followed with her own version: "The length'ning line moves languishing along." "Ms. Wheatley writing in the eighteenth century is simply an imitator of Alexander Pope," charged Amiri Baraka more than a century after the Emancipation Proclamation and more than two centuries after Wheatley's death. "Simply" is exactly the wrong word to describe how Wheatley draws from her influences. Wheatley does not simply imitate Pope. Instead, verse conventions offered her a strategy for survival, the means to prove her humanity and seek her freedom.

As Wheatley's example suggests, the successful use of recognizable artistic conventions can help a poet enter a literature and a culture that seeks to exclude her. It can moderate skepticism, even hostility, and sanction an outsider's admittance into a community. By doing so, it can expand a culture's definitions of its key terms such as *poet*, *genius*, and *humanity*. Those who sought to deny Wheatley's authorship of her poems did so because they recognized literature's authorizing possibility.

In an irony of literary history, the very qualities of Wheatley's poetry that impressed her contemporaries made many readers in later generations dislike it. The force of Wheatley's biblical themes, classical genres (such odes and georgics), and canonical meters relies on the easy familiarity with the literature that educated colonial Americans enjoyed. Later readers are less likely to recognize her allusions, let alone appreciate them. That fact, however, does not diminish Wheatley's technical expertise and mastery of classical genres. Rather, it clarifies how such conventions rely on shared knowledge and taste.

Respect for poetic convention hardly reigns uncontested in American literary culture. With several notable exceptions, American poetry and, even more so, its scholarly discussions value a different quality. American poets and readers alike often appreciate idiosyncrasy and the associated values of disruption, originality, innovation, strangeness, and surprise.

Certain historical and national conditions encouraged this tendency. American poetry developed relatively late in Western literary history. Even as it grew into a major literature, American poetry self-consciously regarded itself as new. Whitman and the poets who followed him recast this potential liability into a strength. American poetry's periods of explosive growth—the nineteenth and early twentieth centuries—coincided with intellectual and literary movements that prized newness and the qualities associated with it. In both its English and its American versions, Romanticism esteemed originality and experimentation. Modernism offered a more aggressive, frantic commitment to these ideals. "Make it new," Pound declared in his famous rallying cry, while Williams insisted, "Nothing is good save the new."

Especially since modernism, poetic idiosyncrasy has often been associated with the need for formal innovation, the creation of new forms and techniques. However, America's most enduringly idiosyncratic poet, Emily Dickinson, almost exclusively wrote in hymn meters, the form she shared with Isaac Watts, whose hymns she read and sang at church. Her poems use convention to interrogate and dislocate it.

Emily Dickinson was born and lived nearly all her life in Amherst, Massachusetts. Amid the Great Revival of 1850, her father, sister, and many friends followed the Calvinist practice of publicly declaring they were saved, but she did not, resisting the pressure to do so. "Christ is calling everyone here, all my companions have answered," she wrote; "I am standing alone in rebellion." While she corresponded with friends and read widely, as an adult she rarely left the family house. When Emerson visited her brother's house next door, Dickinson chose not to meet him. Dickinson published only ten poems during her lifetime. After her death, her sister discovered nearly eighteen hundred handwritten poems folded and sewn together into booklets. When Mabel Loomis Todd and Thomas Wentworth Higginson prepared the poems for publication, a number of issues complicated the process. Most obviously, they found Dickinson's idiosyncratic handwriting difficult to read. Higginson called it "so peculiar that it seemed as if the writer might have taken her first lessons by studying the famous fossil bird-tracks in the museum of that college town." Another issue they faced was Dickinson's frequent and unconventional use of dashes of uneven length and direction. Impressed by the poems, the editors also saw them as enigmatic and technically odd. Higginson called the poems "wayward and unconventional in the last degree; defiant of form, measure, rhyme, and even grammar." "The very absence of conventional form challenges attention," Todd similarly observed.

The editors standardized the poems according to then-current standards, making what Higginson reported as "very few and superficial changes." In fact, they altered fifty of the one hundred poems in the first edition and generally selected Dickinson's least difficult poems. The editors added titles and regularized Dickinson's rhyme, meter, grammar, capitalization, and punctuation (most conspicuously, her frequent use of dashes). For instance, "There's a certain Slant of light, / Winter Afternoons" was changed to "There's a certain slant of light / On winter afternoons" so the second line might keep to the iambic pattern. Some stanzas were dropped (for example, the fourth stanza of "Because I could not stop for Death—").

In addition to his editorial work, Higginson used his contacts to promote and publicize the poems. Published in 1890, four years after Dickinson's death, the poems received a surprising amount of attention, warranting the publication of three editions and one selection of Dickinson's letters in six years. The reviewers had trouble placing Dickinson's poetry, comparing her to nearly one hundred poets in an attempt to find an illuminating parallel or precedent in literary history.

Even more than a century later, Dickinson's poetry remains arrestingly strange, whether viewed in manuscript form (which can be seen online at the Emily Dickinson Archive) or in a modern edition. This effect is not accidental. In her poems and letters, Dickinson insists that art aims to trouble and disquiet: "Nature is a Haunted House—but Art—a House that tries to be haunted." In another letter, Dickinson famously described how poetry achieves this task: "If I read a book [and] it makes my whole body so cold no fire ever can warm me I know that is poetry. If I feel physically as if the top of my head were taken off, I know that is poetry. These are the only way I know it. Is there any other way?"

Dickinson recognizes poetry by its disorienting effect. Instead of naming its formal characteristics or more conventional functions, Dickinson presents a powerfully subjective experience. Words exert a disruptive physical force. Their power is extreme: they make the reader feel a "cold no fire ever can warm" and "as if the top of my head were taken off."

Dickinson's poems use a number of techniques to achieve this effect. At least one-fifth of them are definition poems. They characteristically introduce a formula—"Hope is," "Remorse is," and "Grief is," they start—before turning against the expected clarification, whether by adding a surprising metaphor or personification, a logical leap, or both: for example, "'Hope' is a Thing with Feathers" and "Remorse—is Memory—Awake." Dickinson more than re-examines the terms. She employs a conventional formula to propose a startlingly original, new vocabulary for human experience. Often, the poems qualify the definitions they offer, adding multiple alternatives. By doing so, the definition poems work against the idea that any one stable definition exists. One poem offers five definitions of "grief" in twenty-one lines: "Grief is a Mouse—," "Grief is a Thief—quick startled—," "Grief is a Juggler—boldest at the Play—," "Grief is a Gourmand," and "Best Grief is Tongueless." Deepening the mystery, the "Best Grief" refuses to talk. Described as a martyr for silence, he is burned and tortured in the public square without divulging "a syllable." In a more extreme formulation, some definition poems turn against the very idea of definition. They use a rhetorical structure to challenge it: "The *Definition* of Beauty is, / That definition is none—" and "Its Location / Is Illocality."

The poems also witness inner experience with an unnerving mixture of detachment and intimate intensity. Many describe an internal experience from an external perspective. Perspective does not remain consistent, though. Just as Dickinson's definition poems often refuse to settle for one definition, her poems often switch back and forth from impersonal and more intimate modes of address:

> The Soul selects her own Society—
> Then—shuts the Door—
> To her divine Majority—
> Present no more—
>
> Unmoved—she notes the Chariots—pausing—
> At her low Gate—
> Unmoved—an Emperor be kneeling
> Upon her Mat—
>
> I've known her—from an ample nation—
> Choose One—
> Then—close the Valves of her attention—
> Like Stone—

The poem depicts the soul's exclusive devotion to "One." As in other Dickinson poems (for instance, "I'm Ceded—I've stopped being Theirs—"), the poem opens with an apparently straightforward declaration: "The Soul selects her own Society—." But who exactly is that company whom the soul selects? The early editors added the title, "Exclusion," and early reviewers read the poem autobiographically as Dickinson's declaration of "why she chose her hidden life." More recently, scholars have proposed other possibilities. They describe the poem as addressing the muse, a lover, or God.

The Soul selects her own Society—
then— shuts the Door—
⁺to her Divine Majority—
⁺Present no more—

Unmoved— she notes the Chariots— pausing
At— her low Gate—
Unmoved— an Emperor be kneeling
⁺Upon her Mat—

I've known her— from an Ample
nation—
Choose One—
then— Close the Valves of
her Attention—
Like Stone—

⁺ On ⁺obtrude ⁺ On ⁺ Rush mat— ⁺ lids—

8. Emily Dickinson's handwritten manuscripts challenged her editors
since they were written, as Thomas Wentworth Higginson put it, "in a
handwriting so peculiar that it seemed as if the writer might have
taken her first lessons by studying the famous fossil bird-tracks in the
museum."

The various meanings of the apparently simple phrase "The soul" encourage the divergent readings. Dickinson would not have needed to consult her Webster's dictionary to recognize that the meanings of *soul* range from "the spiritual, rational and immortal substance in man, which distinguishes him from brutes" and whose "immortality," Webster notes, "is a fundamental article of the Christian system" to that definition's much less exulted near opposite, "a human being; a person." The pithy, familiar term shows its flexibility. The capitalization of "One," for example, might seem to support the understanding of the depicted as divine. However, Dickinson also capitalizes its earthly rhyme pair, "Stone." Adding to the complications, the final stanza switches to the first person, "I've known her." The meter also shifts, with the second and fourth lines shortening to one metrical foot, "Chose One" and "Like Stone."

Such ambiguities vex some readers and excite others. In a different context, Adrienne Rich observed that Dickinson "used the Christian metaphor [of twice born] far more than she let it use her." A similar claim might be said of "The Soul selects her own Society—"; it uses Christian language, bending "Soul" to its own multiple uses. Dickinson addresses God as if she were addressing a lover, a lover as if she were addressing God, the Muse as if she were addressing a lover, God, or both. As the final stanza's shift to the first person suggests, the poem might also represent the soul addressing itself. "As always with Emily Dickinson, there can be no final interpretation of the poem," one of Dickinson's keenest readers, the poet Susan Howe, observes. The poem remains both intimate and elusive. What Howe calls Dickinson's "mutable and riddling verse" does not want to be pinned down.

Dickinson and Whitman were contemporaries, though Dickinson showed little interest in Whitman's poetry, admitting to Higginson, "You speak of Mr. Whitman—I never read his Book—but was told that he was disgraceful." Whitman's sprawling free verse offered American poets who followed him a model of how a social vision might be wedded to a poetic form. In this respect, Whitman's poetic form marks a national aspiration. In contrast, Dickinson subverts poetry's foundational techniques, including grammar, verse form, and punctuation, while questioning societal, gender, and theological norms. She uses conventional language and forms far more than they use her. In her open-ended, questioning poems, norms lose their authority.

This subversive quality tends to attract the many poets influenced by Dickinson—Susan Howe, Lucie Brock-Broido, Anne Carson, Heather McHugh, Alice Fulton, and Jorie Graham, to name just a few. Howe, for instance, praises Dickinson's poetry because it "refuses to conform to the Anglo-American literary traditions." Alicia Suskin Ostriker goes a step farther, celebrating Dickinson as "America's first radically experimental poet." As if to validate this point, American poets committed to radical experimentation often claim Dickinson as an important model, crafting poems that echo, quote, and otherwise honor her work.

Dickinson's poetry and the poetry that follows it forcefully suggest that one convention of American poetry is idiosyncrasy. American defenders of poetic convention often must espouse a dissenting view. Writing in the 1930s, the heyday of modernism, Yvor Winters chastised poets for uniformly committing a dire mistake. Winters censured them for falling prey to the "fallacy of expressive, or imitative, form, [that] recurs constantly in modern literature":

> To say that a poet is justified in employing a disintegrating form in order to express a feeling of disintegration, is merely a sophistical justification for bad poetry, akin to the Whitmanian notion that one must write loose and sprawling poetry to "express" the loose and sprawling American continent. In fact, all feeling, if one gives oneself (that is, one's form) up to it, is a way of disintegration; poetic form is by definition a means to arrest the disintegration and order the feeling; and in so far as any poetry tends toward the formless, it fails to be expressive of anything.

It takes Winters less than half a sentence to dismiss much modern poetry criticism as "merely a sophistical justification for bad poetry." Such poetry cannot help but be "bad" since its author fails to recognize and therefore fails to perform their necessary artistic responsibilities. Winters believes that poetic form should not directly express the emotions that the poem explores. Instead, it should retain a certain distance from them, confirming that the poet controls and orders the depicted emotions, not simply giving in to their direct expression. A poem "fails to be expressive of anything" if it cannot keep that distance and formal control.

While many disagreed with the particulars of Winters's combative judgments, many members of the next generation of American poets, the poets starting to publish in the 1950s, crafted metrical verse that employed poetic conventions to related ends. Donald Justice, for instance, described meters' effect in terms that resembled Winters's: "Their very presence seems to testify to some degree of plan, purpose, and meaning...[T]hey have become a conventional sign for at least the desire for some outward control." Justice's elegy for his mother, "Psalm and Lament," describes mourners suffering from a keen loss, but the meter keeps regular time: "The clocks are sorry, the clocks are very sad. / One stops; one goes on striking the wrong hours." The meter testifies to the poet's outward control even amid heartrending grief. As a GI, Anthony Hecht helped to liberate the Flossenburg concentration camp. "The place, the suffering, the prisoners' accounts," he later remembered, "were beyond comprehension." Hecht's Holocaust poems use verse conventions to consider incomprehensible acts; each offers a structure to "arrest the disintegration and order the feeling." "The Book of Yolek," for instance, is a sestina; "It Out-Herods Herod, Pray You Avoid It" is a ballad; and Hecht's sequence "Rites and Ceremonies" includes several intricate rhyming forms.

"In those years," Adrienne Rich later recalled, "formalism was a part of the strategy—like asbestos gloves, it allowed me to handle materials I couldn't pick up barehanded." Rich had her first book accepted for publication while she was still an undergraduate at Radcliffe. *A Change of World* was selected by W. H. Auden for the prestigious Yale Younger Poets Award. In his introduction to the collection, Auden praised Rich's "craftsmanship" in terms that seemed rather reserved if not condescending: "the poems a reader will encounter in this book are neatly and modestly dressed, speak quietly and do not mumble, respect their elders but are not cowed by them, and do not tell fibs." However "neatly and modestly dressed" they may or may not be, Rich's early poems darkly express a foreboding sense of impending doom and confinement. "The glass has been falling all the afternoon" opens "Storm Warnings," while "The Uncle Speaks in the Drawing Room" grimly concludes, "We stand between the dead glass-blowers / And murmurings of missile-throwers." Rich's most anthologized early poem, "Aunt Jennifer's Tigers," presents a niece's horrified observations of her aunt's marriage: "The massive weight of Uncle's wedding band / Sits heavily upon Aunt Jennifer's hand." As perceived by the niece, the wedding band, like the institution of marriage, does not signify love or commitment. It signals ownership: the wedding band Aunt Jennifer wears remains "Uncle's." Death will not end her subjugation. Even in the grave, the aunt will remain "ringed with ordeals she was mastered by."

Rich's early poems display "craftsmanship," the skillful construction of verse in well-established forms, whether the blank verse of "Storm Warnings," the rhyming accentual meter of "The Uncle Speaks in the Drawing Room," or the heroic couplets of "Aunt Jennifer's Tigers." Increasingly, though, Rich explored less familiar forms, inspired by the turbulent political and personal changes she experienced and changing notions of the functions that poetic form should serve. Two years after her college graduation, Rich married, bore three children in four years, and found much of her time and energy consumed with taking care of the children. After a divorce, she continued exploring how to write more directly about her growing political commitments, in particular, her identification as a feminist, lesbian, and antiwar and civil rights activist. "It's exhilarating to be alive in a time of awakening consciousness; it can also be confusing, disorienting, and painful," she observed. Rich started to date her poems in the mid-1950s and publish them with the dates of their composition. "Poetry never stood a chance / of standing outside history," she later asserted. In Rich's terms, dating the poems marked them as self-consciously standing inside history.

"The Burning of Paper Instead of Children" addresses the chaos and violent dislocations of 1968, the year of Robert Kennedy and Martin Luther King's assassinations, the contested Democratic presidential convention, and large antiwar and civil rights protests. Nine antiwar activists, later dubbed the Catonsville Nine, were arrested for burning draft records with napalm. "I was in danger of verbalizing my moral impulses out of existence," Daniel Berrigan, one of the protestors, testified during the trial. Included as the poem's epigraph, Berrigan's explanation introduces the dilemma Rich wrestles with: how to write a poem that expresses her "moral impulses," not verbalizes them "out of existence."

Rich develops several technical strategies to address this challenge. Written in multiple sections, "The Burning of Paper Instead of Children" includes a number of free-verse forms. Line and stanza lengths vary widely. The poem's final section is a prose poem, meaning the poetry is not lineated but organized in a prose paragraph. It also borrows language from the largely Black and Puerto Rican students whom Rich taught in the open admissions program at City College of New York: "Some of the suffering are: it is hard to tell the truth; this is America; I cannot touch you now. In America we have only the present tense. I am in danger. You are in danger. The burning of a book arouses no sensation in me. I know it hurts to burn. There are flames of napalm in Catonsville, Maryland. I know it hurts to burn. The typewriter is overheated, my mouth is burning. I cannot touch you and this is the oppressor's language."

The phrase "The typewriter is overheated" captures the poem's explosive, agitated movement as it leaps from idea to idea, image to image. The poem intermingles a description of erotic frustration ("I cannot touch you") with a more flatly political declaration ("this is America"). Listing both as forms of suffering, the poem rejects the separation of the erotic and the political. Instead, it continues what Rich later called "the work I've been trying to do breaking down the barriers between private and public, the Vietnam War and the lovers' bed."

To accomplish this task, Rich eschews the more impersonal language and poetic forms that her early work favors, which she regarded as overly indebted to male influences and a male-dominated literary tradition. Linking politics, personal history, and verse form, Rich developed an alternative poetics. The form of "The Burning of Paper Instead of Children" expresses a historical and personal sense of fragmentation and confusion. It dramatizes a lack of control, the disorientations that historical change and political trauma bring. The poem also recognizes that Rich writes in "the oppressor's language": in English and within the Anglo-American literary tradition.

Rich's poetic development clarifies a few aspects of the literary values of convention and idiosyncrasy. Convention and idiosyncrasy are not mutually exclusive. In both life and literature, they might not only coexist but also work in concert. As Rich's metaphor of asbestos gloves suggests, her poetry's idiosyncrasy could not exist without the use of familiar forms. The forms' conventionality gave Rich the necessary protection to explore dangerous materials. Similarly, Rich's socially minded poetry searched for solidarity and collaboration even as she developed an alternative poetics to the conventions she was educated in and previously mastered. Second, neither convention nor idiosyncrasy is intrinsically good. What Rich calls "formalism"—the respectful use of preexisting forms—and the creation of new poetic forms offer strategies to address perceived artistic and cultural imperatives. Both face certain risks. At its least successful, idiosyncrasy can be seen as merely puzzling, offering eccentricity merely for its own sake, and convention can seem complacently indebted to outmoded norms.

Idiosyncrasy also faces a historical challenge; the invention of a new technique can quickly turn into a familiar convention. When Rich turned to free-verse techniques, she resembled many of her contemporaries in the 1960s and 1970s who wrote autobiographical free verse. Robert Lowell, for instance, exerted a powerful influence, as his explorations of his mental breakdown and recovery in *Life Studies* and *For the Union Dead* encouraged Sylvia Plath, Anne Sexton, and other poets to explore similar themes. By the 1970s, autobiographical free verse had become the norm in American poetry.

As a consequence, poets interested in disrupting literary norms looked coldly on this technique. "Most American poetry is now written in free verse formats, including much that is fairly straight forward at the level of form," Charles Bernstein observed; "I've always been interested in fractured, demented, asymmetrical, incongruous textures." Motivated by this interest, Bernstein constructed what he called a "prosody of distressed sounds":

We

have preshpas a blurrig of sense, whih
means not relying on convnetionally
methods of *conveying* sense but whih may
aloow for dar greater sense-smakinh than
specisi9usforms of doinat disoucrse that
makes no sense at all by irute of thier
hyperconventionality (Bush's speeches,
calssically).

Compare Bernstein's poetry with my rewriting of it into a more conventional language:

                                               We
          have perhaps a blurring of sense, which
          means not relying on conventional
          methods of *conveying* sense but which may
          allow for far greater sense-making than
          specialized forms of dominant discourse that
          makes no sense at all by virtue of their
          hyper-conventionality (Bush's speeches,
          classically).

Bernstein's poetry disrupts usual methods of reading. In this passage,
he does so mainly by deliberate misspellings, sometimes combined
with violations of grammatical conventions. The poetry distresses
expectations and norms. The third line ends with an adverb,
preparing the reader to expect a verb. The next line, however, begins
with a noun. This language and lineation disorients the reader. To put
this idea in slightly different terms, Bernstein's poetry impedes the
habitual functions of language; he prefers "a blurrig of sense" to
"convnetionally.../ methods of conveying sense."

This strategy presents itself as opposing more than an outworn
literary fashion. The poem contrasts its own unconventionality
with the "hyperconventionality" of "doinat disoucrse." The
speeches of George H. W. Bush, the president of the United States
at the time the poem was written, exemplify this kind of language.
Bernstein clearly disapproves of both Bush's manner of speaking
and his politics and sees both as interconnected, with the failures
of language and logic feeding each other. Through its
unconventionality, poetry—at least the kind of poetry Bernstein
advocates—opposes this political activity. Poetry performs two
connected functions: its innovative techniques challenge
customary modes of reading and perception in order to achieve a
superior form of "sense-making."

Such claims for poetry generated a great deal of scholarly
discussion, often focusing on the question of its political efficacy.

More recently, social media's entrance into nearly all aspects of daily life has made poetry's quick shifts in tone, language, and subject matter feel more like an extension of our customary ways of reading and accessing information than a disruption of them. At least one other reservation should be acknowledged. The commitment to artistic disruption discounts the possibility that clear language might do more than mimic the workings of the dominant discourse. In his novel *The Topeka School*, Ben Lerner wittily concedes that presidential speech has changed, when the mother of the main character, an aspiring poet, describes "how some of the poets you admire sound to me, or I guess what Palin or Trump sound like, delivering nonsense as if it made sense." Writing as a sitting president dashes off misspelled tweets in the early hours of the morning, poets might consider whether their commitment to disjunction that has outlasted several presidential administrations still achieves what they wish, whether this style has hardened into a dogma not sufficiently responsive to the changed linguistic, technological, and political realities.

Even before it was collected in a volume of poetry, Maggie Smith's poem "Good Bones" found an appreciative international audience, propelled by the internet and reprinted abroad. Written before the event, the poem achieved a wide circulation after a mass shooting at Pulse, a gay nightclub in Orlando, Florida. The poem considers a mother's unease trying to protect her children from a full exposure to life's difficulties. "Life is short, though I keep this from my children," the poem opens, before elaborating, "The world is at least / fifty percent terrible, and that's a conservative / estimate, though I keep this from my children." The poem's conclusion returns to the metaphor that the title introduces; the parent feels like a realtor trying to sell a bad house. She is "trying to sell them the world." "Any decent realtor," she observes,

> walking you through a real shithole, chirps on
> about good bones: This place could be beautiful,
> right? You could make this place beautiful.

This poem skillfully follows many free-verse conventions. It plays off repeated phrases (for instance, "I keep this from my children") and words ("beautiful"). Line breaks dramatically revise previous meanings. "This place could be beautiful" offers a promise. "Right?" turns it into a question, a knowing technique to gain the potential buyer's assent. "No good poetry is ever written in a manner twenty years old," Ezra Pound pronounced in a statement often appreciatively cited by those who advocate for the continual production of new verse forms and techniques and dismiss poets not involved in this effort. "Good Bones," a good poem written in a well-established style, calls this judgment into question. It confirms the need for different artistic styles to serve different functions. It shows that poetry might not just disorient and innovate, but also valuably console.

Chapter 4
Auden and Eliot
Two complicating examples

The poetic careers of T. S. Eliot and W. H. Auden trouble the very idea of a national literature. The British-born Auden immigrated to the United States and the American-born Eliot immigrated to England. Both wrote significant poems before and after their moves. In particular, Auden's arrival foreshadowed a notable development that has enlivened the American literary scene from the late 1960s to the present. During this time, many distinguished poets came to America from abroad, including political exiles such as Czeslaw Milosz and Joseph Brodsky and poet-professors such as Eavan Boland, Seamus Heaney, and Derek Walcott, lured by the lucrative teaching opportunities that American universities offered them. (During the 1970–71 academic year, for instance, Seamus Heaney earned a salary nearly three times higher from the University of California, Berkeley, than he earned the previous academic year at Queen's University.) Some of these poets settled in America more or less permanently, whereas others headed back to their home countries nearly as soon as each semester ended. Depending on how one classifies these poets, their presence establishes a paradox: some of the most important poetry written in America may or may not be American poetry.

One can overstate this point in either direction. A poet's address does not define their literary nationality. Instead, a tangled set of family resemblances and allegiances situates the writer and the work. By one scholar's count, William Butler Yeats spent only one-third of his life in Ireland, but generations of readers have hailed him as a great Irish poet, since his poetry remained intimately and passionately concerned with Ireland's fate. "I am of Ireland," he avowed, quoting a fourteenth-century lyric, and addressed "Irish poets" as his colleagues.

It would be equally mistaken simply to ignore the influence that a poet's changed surroundings can exert on their writing. In addition to more conspicuous cross-cultural encounters, to live in another country is to experience language differently, to hear new sounds for the first time, as well as old ones transformed.

Given sound's importance to poetry, subtle shifts can achieve far-reaching consequences. Born and raised in England, Thom Gunn lived nearly his entire adult life in San Francisco but never renounced his British citizenship. Published in 1957, three years after his move to America, "On the Move" describes leather- and goggle-clad motorcyclists imposingly ascending a California hill. The poem's style remains nearly as impersonal as the bikers. The neatly rhyming, metrical stanzas describe them as existential heroes, claiming movement as their identity:

> One joins the movement in a valueless world,
> Choosing it, till, both hurler and the hurled,
> One moves as well, always toward, toward.

"On the Move" also records an English poet in transition, some in ways he may not have realized when he wrote it. Nearly four decades later, Gunn included the poem in his *Collected Poems*, but added an author's note that explained, "Most English people nowadays give 'toward' two syllables whereas Americans, like the Elizabethans, treat it as one. In my early books, I was still an English poet, not yet Anglo American." A glance back at the poem explains the need for this seemingly trivial point. The third line's iambic pentameter scans only if the reader pronounces "toward" as the poet did, not as he soon started to: as an iamb, fully rhyming with the final word in the stanza's second line, "discord." The meter and rhyme scheme depend on this pronunciation; both falter if the poem is read in an American accent. Their fastidiousness requires a way of speaking that the poet will soon discard. Otherwise, it fails.

Even if we were to apply Gunn's somewhat hedging term "Anglo American" to Auden and Eliot, questions still persist about how each author's work engages with the poetry of the country he immigrated to and that of the country he left. One option would be to set these concerns aside and call Auden's and Eliot's poetry "postnational," but that designation largely overlooks how the poets saw themselves, their work, and poetry itself. "No art is more stubbornly national than poetry," Eliot maintained, and he rejected the notion that "English and American poetry" "tend to become merged into one common international type." While Eliot cautioned that he did "not think that a satisfactory statement of what constitutes the difference between an English and an American 'tradition' in poetry could be arrived at," because a counterexample will contradict any generalization, Auden enjoyed creating what he called "cosy little definitions" of the characteristics of the two countries and their poets. These differences not only entertained Auden and his readers; they also inform and, to a certain extent, inspired the poetry he wrote in America.

"There are only two ways in which a writer can become important," Eliot observed, "to write a great deal, and have his writings appear everywhere, or to write very little." Both poets followed Eliot's advice, but in opposite ways. The amount of poetry Eliot wrote was relatively modest (his reputation as a poet rests on roughly 150 pages), but it profoundly influenced modern literature and culture. Few poets writing in English after Eliot could avoid contending with his work. Auden wrote far more prolifically. The multitude of forms and genres he mastered and the breadth of his interests establish his greatness.

An examination of Auden and Eliot's poetry allows us to consider how these two major poets understood American poetry and their place in it, the resources it gave them, and the limitations that frustrated them. Generations of readers have puzzled over these questions because they involve two major authors and the intersections of individual lives with complex issues of nationhood, including national identity, anxiety, and pride. In short, their work enriches the story I have been telling about American poetry by complicating it.

Nearly a quarter century after becoming an English citizen, in 1951 T. S. Eliot returned to his birthplace, St. Louis, Missouri, to deliver a lecture, "American Literature and the American Language." Near its end, the Nobel laureate considered how he might define his own national poetic identity. To draw a contrast, he mentioned the case of W. H. Auden: "Now, I do not know whether Auden is to be considered as an English or as an American poet: his career has been useful to me in providing me with an answer to the same question when asked about myself, for I can say: 'Whichever Auden is, I suppose I must be the other.'" Eliot's quip is evasively instructive. It suggests the complications that quickly arise when trying to place either Eliot or Auden within a specific national literary tradition. Does the poet's artistic national identity simply follow their citizenship? Do they remain forever claimed by the country where they were born? Or can the poet's national identity only be defined in some vague opposition, because they "must be the other"?

Of the two immigrations, Auden's was the more controversial. Auden arrived in America on January 26, 1939; he became a US citizen on May 20, 1946. Thirty-two years old, Auden already enjoyed an international reputation. To many observers, his

9. W. H. Auden (second from right) and T. S. Eliot (center) share a drink at a literary reception. "So long as one was in Eliot's presence," Auden observed, "one felt it was impossible to do or say anything base."

poetry defined the cultural moment that some called, whether in praise or censure, "the age of Auden." Auden's prominence deepened the criticism that he fled his home country imperiled by the rapid approach of war. "When the war broke out, he [Auden] became," Peter Edgerly Firchow observes, "in the eyes of many British contemporaries, not merely an American, but also a renegade and a coward." Adding a biting image to this charge, Evelyn Waugh condemned Auden and his "gang," fellow writers and friends such as Christopher Isherwood and Stephen Spender: "At the first squeak of an air-raid warning the gang dispersed."

The condemnation was not limited to literary circles. It reached the House of Commons, when on June 13, 1940, Major Sir Jocelyn Lucas, MP, rose to ask the parliamentary secretary to the Ministry of Labour whether "British citizens of military age, such as Mr. W. H. Auden and Mr. Christopher Isherwood, who have gone to the United States and expressed their determination not to return to this country until war is over, will be summoned back for registration and calling up, in view of the fact that they are seeking refuge abroad?"

This sense that Auden shamefully shirked his duties also fueled some of the most stinging attacks on his poetry. In his combative review of Auden's 1960 collection, *Homage to Clio*, Philip Larkin divided Auden's oeuvre into poems written before and after 1940, describing them as if written by two different authors: "a tremendously exciting English social poet" and "an engaging, bookish, American talent, too verbose to be memorable and too intellectual to be moving." For Larkin, the outbreak of World War II and Auden's move to America caused "irreparable" harm to Auden's poetry. Auden "lost his key subject and emotion— Europe and the fear of war—and abandoned his audience altogether with their common dialect and concerns." Brandishing "American" as an insult, Larkin describes the cost of Auden's perceived perfidy. The "English" "poet" betrayed his art, nation, and readers, diminishing himself into an "American talent."

Auden, though, shied away from calling himself an American, even after he changed citizenship. Among other reasons, the term struck him as mystifyingly large, especially given America's many racial, geographic, and socioeconomic divisions. "When I hear critics talk of an American art," Auden wrote shortly after his arrival, "I am at a loss to know which America they mean; the America of a Negro janitor in the Bronx is almost as different from the America of a prosperous white farmer in Wisconsin as France is from China."

Instead, Auden defined his national identity more narrowly and wittily. "Who am I now?" he asks in a poem, "An American? No, a New Yorker." In interviews and prose, Auden repeated the point, never renouncing his identity as a New Yorker, even when, in poor health, he left the city to return to live at his alma mater, Christ Church College, Oxford, in the early 1970s. "Though I've lived more than half my life in the States, am an American citizen (which I expect to remain), have acquired a short *a* and that wonderful verb *gotten* and have learned to say *aside from* instead of *apart from*," he noted, "I cannot, of course, call myself an American. I do, however, think of myself as a New Yorker, and believe that I shall continue to think so, even in Oxford."

Following his own self-identification, Auden wrote less as an American than as a New Yorker. The city inspired Auden with its language, architecture, culture, and romantic possibilities. In New York he met and fell in love with Chester Kallman, his companion for the rest of his life. The city also helped him to develop a new poetic identity as he increasingly wrote from the perspective of a particular kind of New Yorker: urbane, cosmopolitan, and prone to homesickness while intensely aware of the contingency and impermanence of any home.

One of the most famous poems Auden wrote shortly after his arrival in America, "September 1, 1939," opens by announcing its New York setting. With a directness that masks a certain caginess, it names the date and the address in Manhattan or, rather, almost names the address:

> I sit in one of the dives
> On Fifty-second Street
> Uncertain and afraid.

The first line uses American slang to introduce a sense of lowness, both physical and psychological. Especially during Prohibition, a dive was often located in a basement, so patrons could "dive" into it without being seen. (The verb, "sit," adds to the image of physical descent.) The low character of those gathered in such places contributes to its seediness. As one study of American vernacular puts it, a dive is "a room in which bad characters meet." As slang, dive would be intelligible to an English audience but also marked by its American origins. It names a disreputable, perhaps even criminal environment while also carrying a fainter association of Hollywood gangster movies.

But what kind of dive does Auden's speaker visit? Auden's reference is both general, "one of the," and specific, "Fifty-second Street." Informed by the address, a little detective work points toward a particular establishment. In his memoir, the poet Harold Norse described how he mentioned "a notorious gay bar called the Dizzy Club on West Fifty-second Street" to Auden, who "loved sleazy dives": "The dive was a sex addict's quick fix [...] From street level you stepped into a tight mass of tight boys in tighter pants. On those sultry August nights it was a sexual experience just getting a drink." According to Norse, Auden visited the Dizzy Club the following night, September 1, 1939, and wrote the poem there on that date.

Impersonal and intimate, the opening lines feature an anonymous speaker ruminating on a moment of historical rupture with a kind of coded language. Setting a poem in America, Auden turns to American slang, which enlivens the otherwise flatly descriptive opening two lines, the journalistic recitation of the facts.

While the American slang belongs to the depicted New York scene, it also distances the speaker from it. Auden loved nearly all kinds of language. Later in his career, he voraciously mined the unabridged *Oxford English Dictionary* for promising words to use in his poetry. (The dictionary returned Auden's affection; it currently cites 769 examples from his work, including the opening lines of "September 1, 1939.") Those poems delight in linguistic rarities such as *cumber*, *osse*, and *blithe* (as a verb). In this respect,

America offered Auden a new supply of words. Auden's use of its slang, though, often sounds not quite natural. The reference to "dive" is meant to establish a knowing toughness, but the speaker of "September 1, 1939" sounds like someone trying out a new way of talking. The opening lines, Joseph Brodsky observe, have the "distinct air of a reporting.... He [the poet] is a newsman reporting to his people back in England." Auden wrote from New York in a language borrowed from that place, but it does not seem to fully belong to him. Paradoxically, the American slang indicates the speaker's remove from the scene he inhabits.

The line's meter adds to the effect. The opening is trimeter; each line contains three stresses.

> /　　/　　/
> I sit in one of the dives
> 　/　　/　　/
> On Fifty-second Street
> 　/　　　/　　/
> Uncertain and afraid...

Auden borrowed this meter from William Butler Yeats's "Easter 1916," Yeats's meditation on the failed Irish rebellion.

> 　/　　　/　　/
> I have met them at close of day
> /　　　/　/
> Coming with vivid faces
> /　　　/　　　/
> From counter or desk among grey...

Auden had been thinking deeply about Yeats in the months before he wrote "September 1, 1939." Only a few days after Auden arrived in New York, he learned that Yeats had died. Moved by the occasion, he quickly elegized Yeats in the first poem he wrote in America, "In Memory of W. B. Yeats." Yeats, however, offered

Auden a difficult model. Auden praised Yeats as "a consummate master" of "diction," a poetic element Auden ranked higher than "subject-matter or wisdom." Their politics, however, clashed. Yeats's poetry, Auden observed, "shows scant sympathy with the Social Consciousness of the Thirties," the politics that Auden and his circle espoused. Instead, Yeats's reactionary leanings led Auden to speculate that, had World War II broken out earlier and had Germany invaded Ireland, Yeats might have willingly collaborated with the Nazis.

In addition to borrowing Yeats's meter, Auden also expanded an American version of one of Yeats's scenes. "Easter 1916" briefly mentions "a mocking tale or a jibe / To please a companion / Around the fire at the club." Auden's silent drinkers, "faces along the bar," gather in a dive, not a club, desperately lonely but eager to avoid seeing themselves as they are, "Children afraid of the night / Who have never been happy or good."

At the time that Auden wrote "September 1, 1939," the distinction he increasingly drew between New York and America had not yet hardened. Setting the poem in New York, Auden explored what he saw as American literature's great theme and one of the culture's defining characteristics. "During my short residence here," Auden observed in 1940, "I have come to feel that most Americans are profoundly lonely, and that in this more than in anything else lies the explanation of American violence." "The American literary tradition," Auden added a year later, "is a literature of lonely people."

"September 1, 1939" joins this literary tradition. Its Americanness deepens the depicted loneliness. For example, the bar's design follows an American model, not the British or Irish. Unlike drinkers in a British pub or Irish "companion[s] / Around the fire at the club," the "faces along the bar" do not face each other. Instead, they stare at their own reflections in the mirror above the bar. No one shares even "a mocking tale or a jibe" with a "companion," let alone a kind word. In such places, happiness seems nearly impossible.

Auden's use of a borrowed verse line mitigates the depicted loneliness. The echo connects the poem to something beyond itself, to a precedent as well as an inspiration. It places Auden's poem in the company of Yeats as the two poets share the three-stress line. Writing amid the failed Easter Rebellion, Yeats struggled to foresee what might follow it: "All changed, changed utterly: / A terrible beauty is born." Faced with another moment of great transformation and confusion, Auden borrows Yeats's meter to advocate the need for universal love based in an understanding of all humanity's interdependence, since "no one exists alone":

> Hunger allows no choice
> To the citizen or the police;
> We must love one another or die.

When quoted by graduation speakers or politicians, the last line's rousing exhortation sweetens some of the passage's bitter logic. The qualifications, though, need to be remembered. Dire need, not preference, unites humanity. The examples Auden offers to illustrate this idea suggest how much division marks humankind. When naming two groups that need to learn to love each other, Auden does not mention "the criminal or the police," two groups perhaps naturally antagonistic to each other. Instead, "September 1, 1939" assumes that even in a democracy such as America, the citizen and the police regard each other with deep suspicion, if not hostility.

The poem's most famous line, "We must love one another or die," though, deeply frustrated Auden. According to his account, he reworked it before discarding the whole poem as unsalvageable. Rereading the line, Auden "said to myself: 'That's a damned lie! We must die anyway.' So, in the next edition, I altered it to

> We must love one another and die.

"This didn't seem to do either, so I cut the whole stanza. Still no good. The whole poem, I realized, was infected with an incurable dishonesty and must be scrapped."

Auden's rather hefty *Collected Poems* contains nearly nine hundred pages of poetry, but not "September 1, 1939," although the poem remains immensely popular and widely admired. Following Auden's wishes, his literary executor excluded the poem. The defective line and the poem it "infected" bothered Auden not because he considered it to be awkwardly worded or inaccurate. Auden disavowed "September 1, 1939" because he believed it committed a more serious offense.

For Auden, the poem's failing repeated the chief failing of the age, what "September 1, 1939" calls "a low dishonest decade." Auden thought this mendacity not only marked the 1930s, whose moral failings allowed fascism to rise and another world war to start, but also associated it with England, as he explained in a letter to a friend he drafted but did not send: "The reason (artistic) I left England and went to the U.S. was precisely to stop me writing poems like 'Sept. 1st, 1939' the most dishonest poem I have ever written. A hang-over from the U.K. It takes time to cure oneself." Auden does not say how England inspired this poetic dishonesty, only that it necessitated his move to America.

In another poem Auden wrote shortly after his move, "Refugee Blues," New York represents America: immensely large but wracked with class divisions and cruelly indifferent to suffering. In a vivid illustration of the human costs of these contradictions, German Jews fleeing Nazi persecution find themselves barred from entering the city and finding safety. At times, the poem bluntly specifies the danger that the refugees face, describing, "Hitler over Europe, saying: 'They must die.'" Despite its vast resources, though, New York refuses to help the couple fleeing their death sentence:

> Say this city has ten million souls,
> Some are living in mansions, some are living in holes:
> Yet there's no place for us, my dear, yet there's no place for us.

While "September 1, 1939" sets American slang in a form borrowed from Yeats, "Refugee Blues" uses an African American form, the blues, but largely avoids the language associated with that tradition. The first stanza incorporates, at most, a few light touches of the blues idiom: the syntax that "say" introduces and, perhaps, the slang of "holes." Instead, Auden adapts the blues form's traditions. He imitates the effects that its features achieve without strictly replicating the formal elements.

In particular, Auden's tercets vary the structural elements of the classic blues stanza. Though other versions exist, blues stanzas often consist of three lines, with the first two repeating and the third rhyming with them. In contrast, the first two lines of Auden's tercets rhyme, "souls" and "holes," but the final line, ending in "us," does not. Instead of the second line "worrying" the first line, varying it slightly, the second line worries the repeated phrase, "Some are living." In this respect, Auden follows what one scholar has called "the blues logic," the music's call and response, even though Auden adjusts the particulars of its structure.

A comparison with Langston Hughes's blues poetry clarifies Auden's method. In "Homesick Blues," Hughes stays closer to the blues tradition:

> I went down to the station.
> My heart was in ma mouth.
> Went down to the station.
> Heart was in ma mouth.
> Lookin' for a box car
> To roll me to de South.

Writing words meant to be read on the page, not sung, Hughes splits the classic blues line in half, breaking three lines into six. He uses lineation to approximate the effect that a blues singer achieves when they pause midline. "I went down to the station. / My heart was in ma mouth," Hughes writes, not, "I went down to the station. My heart was in ma mouth."

"Homesick Blues" more straightforwardly employs other blues conventions, including well-established structures, language, themes, and motifs. It rhymes according to the blues' most common pattern; the first two lines' last word, "mouth," rhymes with its counterpart in the concluding line, "South." Hughes's imagery and themes remain similarly traditional. Returning to the blues' great theme of Southern migration, Hughes illustrates it with its canonical expression, the image of a train, which, as Albert Murray notes, achieved a "mythological" status in "the experience and hence the imagination of so-called black southerners."

Hughes's "Homesick Blues" also adheres to the blues' common argumentative structure. As in many blues songs, the final line in each stanza movement responds to the ideas or emotions that the opening two lines express. The last lines of Hughes's blues poems variously illuminate, justify, or contradict the lines they follow. In "Homesick Blues," the last line explains the lines that precede it. "Lookin' for a box car / To roll me to de South" names the cause of the speaker's sadness, why he "went down to the station. / My heart was in ma mouth."

In contrast, "Refugee Blues" more alludes to the blues than commits to its formal properties. The poem's remove from the musical tradition can be seen most clearly when its language sounds decidedly unlike the blues:

> In the village churchyard there grows an old yew,
> Every spring it blossoms anew;
> Old passports can't do that, my dear, old passports can't do that.

and:

> Went down to the harbour and stood upon the quay,
> Saw the fish swimming as if they were free:
> Only ten feet away, my dear, only ten feet away.

Some readers find British spellings and phrasings such as "harbour" and "upon the quay" strange for a blues poem. Expressing this reservation, one scholar calls "Refugee Blues" "a funny hybrid" of "the blues" and "an undeniable British idiom."

The tension between these elements, though, strikes me as productive, even poignant. Auden strikes a delicate balance, avoiding an appropriation that approaches blackface. "Refugee Blues" describes the plight of German Jews barred from entering New York. Appropriately, they do not sound like Americans or, more specifically, African Americans, let alone like blues musicians. Instead, their language reflects their status as stateless people burdened with "old passports." The differences between "harbour" and "harbor," "quay" and "dock," are slight but significant. These makers identify a speaker as native or foreign to a particular place, whether in a blues poem or an immigration office. In the case of the refugees, their language suggests the small differences that condemn them to a terrible fate, their particular foreignness that keeps them painfully "only ten feet away" from freedom.

At the same time, the blues form, one of America's great artistic inventions, allows Auden to explore his new national identity. Tellingly, the majority of the stanzas develop an antithesis between its first two lines and the concluding line. The "city" houses "ten million souls," rich and poor, the opening lines announce, but it has "no place" for the refugees, the last line counters. The series of antitheses that Auden crafts speaks to a larger ambivalence about the freedoms and opportunities that New York offers him. He writes as a newcomer to the city, an immigrant with the right passport, lamenting his new hometown's heartlessness to those who do not.

Both written within months of Auden's arrival in the United States, "September 1, 1939" and "Refugee Blues" might be called transitional poems in the sense that they record Auden working out his new identity in New York. Auden's later and more lighthearted poem, "On the Circuit," firmly builds on his distinction between an American and a New Yorker. Published in 1963, it describes an increasingly popular phenomenon, the poetry tour, where a well-known poet flies to a number of locations and reads their work. The America outside New York exists in a blur, "Massachusetts, Michigan, / Miami or L.A.," only partly for the reason that the speaker acknowledges:

> I shift so frequently, so fast,
> I cannot now say where I was
> The evening before last.

Even more than the hectic schedule, the speaker barely remembers the places he visits and the people he meets there because he has little interest in either. Instead, the touring poet presents himself as crochety middle aged, "homesick for our snug / Apartment in New York" and disinclined to appreciate nearly anything outside it. "A sulky fifty-six, he finds / A change of mealtime utter hell," the poet grumbles. Accordingly, he most keenly observes the annoyances that befall him, such as

> The radio in students' cars,
> Muzak at breakfast, or—dear God!—
> Girl-organists in bars.

The poem ends with a mock prayer that appropriates the public language of patriotic American religiosity:

> God bless the lot of them, although
> I don't remember which was which:
> God bless the U.S.A., so large,
> So friendly, and so rich.

The first line is especially evocative. It opens with the stock phrase of American politicians, "God bless," but before completing it with "the U.S.A.," Auden switches out of an American idiom and into an English one, "the lot of them." Allowing the comic anticipation to build, the speaker gives the impression that he needs a moment to prepare himself to utter the disagreeable cliché, "God bless the U.S.A." Of course, when he does, he adds a backhand compliment, commending America for the money it lavishes on its visiting poets, as if "the U.S.A." deserves praise for little else.

As in "September 1, 1939," Auden addresses an audience outside "the U.S.A.," but, this time, to his lover back in "our snug / Apartment in New York," not his readership in England. He is a New Yorker reporting to those back home. If Auden insults those he meets on tour, he also charms them. In "On the Circuit," Auden plays Auden, an English-born New Yorker lost in a doubly foreign culture, grumpy but not mean, partly because he acknowledges his own eccentricities. The English language's last master of light verse, Auden realizes verse form's power to insult but not wound. His handling of meter and rhyme lightens the poem's tone. From schoolyard taunts to hip-hop, rhymes powerfully intensify an attack's force. They add bite and ferocity. "On the Circuit" works differently. Auden's sociable verse technique encourages even those the poem mocks to laugh. It more connects strangers than reinforces antipathies, inviting, not alienating. Recounting his travels through a country he found "profoundly lonely," Auden resists contributing to its "literature of lonely people." Instead, his humor reduces the loneliness he encounters. Even when complaining about his hosts, he sounds like good company.

In 1914, Ezra Pound wrote to Harriet Monroe, the editor of *Poetry* magazine, to recommend the work of a fellow American expatriate Pound recently met in London:

> He has sent in the best poem I have yet had or seen from an
> American. PRAY GOD IT BE NOT A SINGLE AND UNIQUE

SUCCESS. He has taken it back to get it ready for the press and you shall have it in a few days.

He is the only American I know of who has made what I call adequate preparations for his writing. He has actually trained himself *and* modernized himself *on his own*. The rest of the promising young have done one or the other but never both (most of the swine have done neither). It is such a comfort to meet a man and not have to tell him to wash his face, wipe his feet, and remember the date (1914) on the calendar.

At the time, T. S. Eliot was a Harvard graduate student abroad on a fellowship, unhappily reading philosophy for the year at Oxford. An aspiring author, he was unknown and virtually unpublished.

Writing to Monroe, Pound promoted more than a poem; he promoted a new way of writing. Pound recommended the unnamed poem because it was modern, responsive to its historical moment, "the date (1914) on the calendar." To write a poem equal to this fact requires significant work, what Pound calls "adequate preparations."

After a few more rounds of Pound's salesmanship, Monroe gave in to Pound's appeals and published the poem, "The Love Song of J. Alfred Prufrock." Eliot's poem opens:

> Let us go then, you and I,
> When the evening is spread out against the sky
> Like a patient etherized upon a table;
> Let us go, through certain half-deserted streets,
> The muttering retreats
> Of restless nights in one-night cheap hotels
> And sawdust restaurants with oyster-shells:
> Streets that follow like a tedious argument
> Of insidious intent
> To lead you to an overwhelming question…
> Oh, do not ask, "What is it?"
> Let us go and make our visit.

The opening two lines extend a romantic invitation, which the third line shockingly turns against. The simile likens the gentle sights of an evening stroll to a patient undergoing an operation, cut open and examined by near strangers. The body is "spread out" so surgeons can work on it. The exposed flesh causes concern, fear, and embarrassment; it does not inspire pleasure. In later parts of the poem, Prufrock expresses his apprehension that others will mock the "bald spot in the middle of my hair" and his "thin" "arms and legs." In Prufrock's self-view, he resembles the "patient etherized upon a table" because the most notable features of his body are its flaws. In the simile, the poem drops from the sky to the table, the ethereal to the bodily, the romantic to the unhealthy, the pleasurable to the unpleasant. The medical term, "etherized," adds a corresponding jarring shift in diction, moving from the language of romantic verse to that of medicine.

Adding to the effect, Eliot's metrically irregular lines convey a nervous energy as they describe sordid city streets, "restless nights in one-night cheap hotels." "The ghost of some simple metre," Eliot asserted, "should lurk behind the arras in even the 'freest' verse; to advance menacingly as we doze, and withdraw as we rouse." Eliot called this kind of poetry *verse libre*, meaning liberated verse, as it neither sets aside a meter (as in free verse) nor commits to one (as in metrical verse). Instead, Eliot's *verse libre* lines skittishly advance and withdraw from iambic pentameter; they do not settle into any stable pattern or its clear absence. The irregularly spaced rhymes add to the jittery, unnerving effect.

Quickly these techniques grew into commonplaces. Eliot's influence can clearly be heard in a poem that William Faulkner wrote less than a decade later:

> We will go alone, my soul and I,
> To a hollow cadence down this neutral street;
> To a rhythm of feet
> Now stilled and fallen. I will walk alone...

Faulkner borrowed his lines' "hollow cadence" and much of their language and syntax from Eliot. Faulkner presents a Prufrock-like speaker in *verse libre*. In addition to the poem's numerous verbal echoes, Faulkner barely revises the opening of "Prufrock," "Let us go then, you and I," into his ersatz version, "We will go alone, my soul and I."

The influence of "The Love Song of J. Alfred Prufrock" subsequently crossed generations. "With this line, modern poetry begins," John Berryman proclaimed of the third line, "Like a patient etherized upon a table." The disorienting simile undercuts the romantic opening. Berryman celebrated it for inaugurating modern poetry because it introduced a new dynamic between poet and reader, in which the poet forcefully undermined the reader's expectations. Instead of "sitting down to entertain, beguile, charm, and lull a reader," modern poets followed Eliot by offering "obstacles and surprise." They made their reader do what Berryman called a "double-take."

Prufrock's third line echoed throughout modern culture as generations of poets and artists challenged their audiences with feinting works that turned against the expectations they aroused. It helped Auden to write, "Lay your sleeping head, my love, / Human on my faithless arm," and, more distantly, Bob Dylan to sing, "Yes, I wish that for just one time you could stand inside my shoes. / You'd know what a drag it is to see you," and Kurt Cobain to sneer, "I wish I was like you, easily amused." All start with apparently sincere expressions, whether a tender invitation ("Lay your sleeping head, my love"), a plea for empathy ("Yes, I wish that for just one time you could stand inside my shoes"), or a compliment ("I wish I was like you"), but swiftly dismiss anyone who believes them. Auden modifies the romantic opening with two adjectives that cynically depict the lovers as deeply flawed and dishonest, "Human on my faithless arm," and Dylan and Cobain transform near-clichés of mutual understanding and respect into rather biting insults.

Eliot started "The Love Song of J. Alfred Prufrock" while a
Harvard undergraduate. As an aspiring poet, Eliot found
American poetry lacking; "there were no American poets at all," he
later dismissively recounted. Instead, he largely turned to the
work of poets outside the English language for his poetic training.
Two French poets offered him particularly useful models. "I think
that from Baudelaire I learned first, a precedent for the poetical
possibilities, never developed by any poet writing in my own
language, of the more sordid aspects of the modern metropolis,"
he remembered while crediting Jules Laforgue for being "the first
to teach me how to speak," namely, employ the jagged, ironic *verse
libre* line of "Prufrock."

These influences made his readers struggle to place the poetry.
"My own verse, if I remember, was at first appreciated in England
because it seemed very American," he recalled, "whereas in
America it did not strike people as being American, but rather as
being French: in neither place did it fit in to the 'tradition.'" Such
confusions only increased with the decades Eliot spent abroad.
After a year at Oxford, Eliot moved to London, dismissing
"modern philosophy" as "nothing more than a logomachy."
Entering literary circles, he eked out a meager living, supporting
himself as a teacher, a reviewer, a banker, and eventually an editor,
while building his reputation as his generation's leading poet and
critic. In 1929, he became a British citizen, after earlier that year
privately converting to the Church of England, a decision that
shocked many in the literary world. Eliot lived the rest of his life
in England, visiting America frequently. Contending with these
facts, Eliot himself puzzled over his national status as a poet.
Decades after he became a British citizen, he signed a review with
the Greek term for resident alien, *Metoikos*. "I am an English poet
of American origin," he wrote on another occasion, then scratched
out the sentence.

Eliot's most famous poem, "The Waste Land," avoids the American
landscape and vernacular. Instead, it remains largely set in

London, the "Unreal City," where Eliot lived and worked while venturing into other European locales. It also presents the reader with a new, distinctively challenging kind of poetry. According to Eliot, the twentieth century demanded poems equal to the age's "variety and complexity." "Poets in our civilization, as it exists at present, must be *difficult*," Eliot asserted, explaining: "Our civilization comprehends great variety and complexity, and this variety and complexity, playing upon a refined sensibility, must produce various and complex results. The poet must become more and more comprehensive, more allusive, more indirect, in order to force, to dislocate if necessary, language into his meaning."

Eliot, however, did not seek to baffle readers needlessly. To help them navigate the "allusive" and "indirect" poem (as well as guard against the charge of plagiarism), "The Waste Land" includes Eliot's endnotes, which name many of its sources and allusions.

All of these qualities—the poem's foreboding difficulty, its conspicuous erudition, and its apparent remove from America— enraged William Carlos Williams. Objecting to the poem, Williams described Eliot as his artistic enemy and likened "The Waste Land" to a weapon of mass destruction. Williams reported that "The Waste Land" made him feel as if "an atom bomb had been dropped upon it and our brave sallies into the unknown were turned to dust....Critically Eliot returned us to the classroom." Williams advocated for "a new art form" "rooted in the locality which should give it fruit." As Williams saw it, Eliot's poetry instead ripped out these roots. Explaining William's hostility, his publisher, James Laughlin, notes that Williams regarded Eliot as "A traitor who had left his / Country and its culture to go / Over to the British."

"The Waste Land" opens far from America, with an image of life in death, set, incongruously, in spring:

> April is the cruellest month, breeding
> Lilacs out of the dead land, mixing

> Memory and desire, stirring
> Dull roots with spring rain.
> Winter kept us warm, covering
> Earth in forgetful snow, feeding
> A little life with dried tubers.

This description of a European landscape (the following lines mention a German lake) reverses the famous prologue of Chaucer's medieval epic, *The Canterbury Tales*: "Whan that aprill with his shoures soote / The droghte of march hath perced to the roote, ..." Instead of regeneration, pilgrimage, and pleasure, spring brings a morbid combination of painful dissatisfactions, "mixing / Memory and desire."

The poem's allusions intensify until fragments jostle against each other in the last section's concluding lines:

> I sat upon the shore
> Fishing, with the arid plain behind me
> Shall I at least set my lands in order?
> London Bridge is falling down falling down falling down
> *Poi s'ascose nel foco che gli affina*
> *Quando fiam uti chelidon*—O swallow swallow
> *Le Prince d'Aquitaine à la tour abolie*
> These fragments I have shored against my ruins
> Why then Ile fit you. Hieronymo's mad againe.
> Datta. Dayadhvam. Damyata.
> Shantih   shantih   shantih

This passage includes at least nine scenes across nine time periods in five languages. The vast majority consist of brief quotations taken from sources as diverse as a traditional nursery rhyme, Dante's *Purgatory*, the Philomela legend, and Thomas Kyd's *The Spanish Tragedy*. According to Eliot's endnotes, the repetition of "Shantih" serves "a formal ending to an Upanishad," meaning "The Peace which passeth understanding."

The key explanatory line, though, remains neither a quotation nor a reference but the unpunctuated sentence Eliot crafted out of his own words, "These fragments I have shored against my ruins." Eliot wrote the last two sections of "The Waste Land" in a sanatorium in Switzerland, recovering from a nervous breakdown. The poem's ferocious concluding movement might be read as a desperate search for a unity, a cobbling together of remembered lines and memories, shards of language and their associations. Many of the lines return to images of destruction and collapse, whether of London Bridge or the prince in the ruined tower. The repetition of "Shantih" mysteriously restores a sense of peace and wholeness, one beyond human understanding.

The "fragments" "shored against my ruins" also record a distinctly artistic effort: the struggle to construct a new literary tradition, to cobble together usable precedents from the past into a new order and a contemporaneous whole. Eliot advocated for the importance of "tradition," though he bristled at its usual definitions. Instead, he believed that a poet must have "a feeling that the whole of the literature of Europe from Homer and within it the whole of the literature of his own country has a simultaneous existence and composes a simultaneous order." "Tradition," Eliot rather confidently declared, "cannot be inherited, and if you want it you must obtain it by great labour." This observation describes nothing so well as Eliot's own poetry, as canonical and obscure authors speak to each other across centuries and languages, both timeless and timely.

Paradoxically, Eliot sounds most American when he asserts his connection to "the whole of the literature of Europe." In an essay on American poetry, Auden noted that European poets differ from American poets, as "every European poet, I believe, still instinctively thinks of himself as a 'clerk,' a member of a professional brotherhood, with a certain social status...and as taking his place in an unbroken historical succession." In contrast, "every American poet feels that the whole responsibility for contemporary poetry has fallen on his shoulders, that he is a literary aristocracy of one." For this reason, Eliot's emphasis on the "great labour" a poet must exert to obtain a tradition "would seem strange" to a European poet. Auden's last point is especially revealing. To rephrase it a bit, an American poet thinks of himself as exceptional, even when, like Eliot, he defends "tradition." The American belief in novelty rests so deeply within Eliot, he cannot conceive of an author simply inheriting a tradition; he must create it from the wreckage of the past and the scattered possibilities of the present. Instead, Eliot retains—as Ralph Ellison observed—a "kind of irreverent reverence which Americans are apt to have for the good products of the past." Eliot's very notion of tradition betrays the American emphasis on innovation and newness, even when he apparently argues against it.

English-born observers liked to prick Eliot by noting when his displays of Englishness revealed an ignorance of the country's manners and history. They recounted the small missteps that happened when, at least as they saw it, "Eliot forgot he was an American." Richard Aldington, for instance, described walking with Eliot in London nearly a decade after Eliot moved there: "To my horror Eliot lifted his derby hat to the sentry outside Marlborough House. You would have to be born British and serve in the army to understand the complex violations of etiquette involved in this generous and well-meant gesture."

In a subtler observation, Auden noted an incongruous detail in "The Waste Land." "I'm sure, for example, that one would immediately detect a difference between poems written about Nature by English poets and by American," Auden claimed. "Thus the opening words of *The Waste Land*, 'April is the cruellest month,' could not possibly have been written by anyone brought up in England. The American climate, outside of California, is violent, the English is mild."

Certainly, one might quibble with Auden's claim. After all, a poet can imagine a climate other than that of his native country, and a nation as vast as America contains a variety of climates. Even with these reservations in mind, Auden usefully reminds us how tenacious our national identities remain, how they inflect our speech, manners, and imagination in ways we might not realize, though these markers appear obvious to observers. Even though some may long for a postnational world, national identity retains a formidable claim on us. Recognizing this fact, Eliot described poets' literary nationalities as a matter beyond choice and language, something we carry with us, no matter where we live. "The American writing in English does not write English poetry," Eliot observed. "It is not the trying to be American or Irish that does it, nor is it the choice of local subject matter, fundamentally; it is the different rhythm in the blood."

Eliot's last major poem, "Four Quartets," returns to the intimate connection between a native landscape and the "rhythm in the blood." "In my beginning is my end," the poem repeats, exploring the question of where and when this beginning takes place. One section, "The Dry Salvages," describes a personal beginning, the Mississippi River of Eliot's St. Louis boyhood and the Massachusetts coast where Eliot summered as a boy: "The river is within us, the sea is all about us."

Another section, "East Coker," moves further back in time, revisiting Eliot's ancestral home, the village that Eliot's direct ancestor Andrew Eliot left to immigrate to America in the seventeenth century. In a moving passage, the poem approaches a wedding celebration held in an open field, first recognized by folk music performed on modest instruments:

> If you do not come too close, if you do not come too close,
> On a summer midnight, you can hear the music
> Of the weak pipe and the little drum.

As the poem's perspective draws nearer, dancers are seen, circling the fire, "holding eche other by the hand or the arm":

> And see them dancing around the bonfire
> The association of man and woman
> In daunsinge, signifying matrimonie—

This tender description of a village celebrating a summer wedding feels a world away from "The Waste Land." "The Waste Land" describes fertility as cruel, "breeding / Lilacs out of the dead land," and sex as painfully sordid, diseased, and exploitative. In a harrowing scene, "the young man carbuncular" "assaults" the "typist," leaving her apartment with "one final patronising kiss." "Well now that's done: and I'm glad it's over," afterward she thinks. In contrast, "East Coker" calls marriage "a dignified and commodious sacrament" and its consummation, like the movement of the dancers, joyful and holy. A change of style matches the change in sentiment. Fragments do not dislocate language into meaning. Instead, the description gracefully follows the unpretentious, mirthful dancers "leaping through the flames."

Less than a decade and a half after his baptism confirmed him in the Church of England, the middle-aged Eliot expressed his Christian faith, not his disgust over modern depravity. The language he employs deepens his connection to East Coker. Eliot borrows phrases from a sixteenth-century treatise written by his direct ancestor, Sir Thomas Elyot. Deliberately, Eliot kept Elyot's spelling, rejecting the advice of those who advised him to modernize it. "The lines in archaic spelling," Eliot explained, "have the purpose of localising in time the fairy-like vision." The sixteenth-century spelling returns language to the moment and the place the poem depicts. It locates the poem in Eliot's ancestral home centuries before he was born, helping, as Eliot observed, "to give the imagery in that section a local habitation in time."

The poem, though, does not fully enter the scene it witnesses; it does not completely return to its "beginning." "If you do not come too close, if you do not come too close," "East Coker" repeats, warning that a certain distance from the dancers and the musicians must be maintained. Even in this welcoming vision, the past remains separate from the present; ancestors and descendants do not mix. To put this idea in national terms, T. S. Eliot experiences this very English scene as an American, quoting historical documents, admiring the dance but not joining it.

Chapter 5
On the present and future of American poetry

In 1957, Elizabeth Bishop wrote to Robert Lowell to express her admiration for the poems he had sent her: "I am green with envy with your kind of assurance. I feel that I could write in as much detail about my Uncle Artie, say—but what would be the significance? Nothing at all.... Whereas all you have to do is put down the names! And the fact that it seems significant, illustrative, American, etc., gives you, I think, the confidence you display about tackling any idea or theme, seriously, in both writing and conversation."

What made those names "significant, illustrative, American, etc."? In the poems he shared with Bishop, Lowell wrote about his family: his mother, father, and maternal uncle, all of whom bore names that identified them as members of New England's oldest families: the Lowells (his father's side) who arrived in America in 1639, and the Winslows (his mother's) who arrived on the Mayflower. Together, their ancestors included two governors of Plimouth Plantation, several notable poets (including James Russell Lowell and Amy Lowell), colonial governors, and leading figures in academia, the military, judiciary, and business.

Especially in New England, the poet's home region, the name Lowell inescapably summons a formidable history. Lowell grew up in Boston, a short drive to a city, Lowell, Massachusetts, named for one ancestor; he attended a college with a residential house, Harvard's Lowell House, named for another, a former president of the university. As a student at St. Mark's School, where his great-grandfather, another Lowell, had been headmaster, he endured his classmates relentlessly teasing him with the famous rhyme that used his last name as a symbol of Brahmin exclusivity, "good old Boston," "Where the Lowells talk to the Cabots, / And the Cabots talk only to God."

Lowell's immediate family, though, was neither wealthy nor particularly distinguished. "Ours was an old family. It stood—just," Lowell told an interviewer, giving its "English equivalent" as "the Duke of Something's sixth cousins." In the poems Bishop admired, Lowell uses family names to highlight that attenuated state. "He smiled his oval Lowell smile," one poem notes of the poet's terminally ill father. Set after both parents' deaths, another poem, "Sailing Home from Rapallo," emphasizes the pathetic particulars of his mother's funeral. Scanning the family plot, the speaker observes his father's grave: "The only 'unhistoric' soul to come here / was Father" buried amid "Mother's relatives: / twenty or thirty Winslows and Starks." Lowell's father—"a gentle, faithful and dim man," as the poet calls him elsewhere—is assigned a singularly negative status as "the only unhistoric soul": not merely the most recently deceased but a Lowell of low accomplishment, unheroic, and dwarfed by his and his wife's family histories. In a cruel touch, the poem quotes the "Lowell motto: *Occasionem cognosce*" (recognize opportunity) carved on the father's tombstone, another reminder of the inherited standard he failed to meet.

"Sailing Home from Rapallo" culminates in one last diminishment of the Lowell name: "In the grandiloquent lettering on Mother's coffin, / *Lowell* had been misspelled *LOVEL*." Bishop's point speaks exactly to this kind of detail. The Lowell name charges a seemingly small, albeit regrettable mistake with significance. If the poem had been written about nearly any other family, or to, to use Bishop's example, her "Uncle Artie," the misspelling would seem carelessly inconsiderate. The Lowell family's long, prominent involvement in America and American history adds to the detail's weight. It shows how far the name has fallen, misspelled in "grandiloquent lettering" on the coffin, reduced to a gaudy, embarrassing defacement.

One marker of how American poetry has changed over the past few decades are the names it regards as important. In a quirk of literary history, the Boston Brahmin's work offered mid-century American poets not born with grand family names a useful model to explore their own obsessions and experiences. To borrow Bishop's term, they gained confidence from his example. Collected in his 1959 book, *Life Studies*, Lowell's poems encouraged an autobiographical turn in American poetry. A generation of poets, including Sylvia Plath, Anne Sexton, John Berryman, and W. D. Snodgrass, considered agonizing personal matters such as divorce, psychological breakdown, and suicide, often (but not always) in seemingly casual free verse and set in the context of the Cold War.

The contemporary poets who follow Lowell's model of blending public and private history, though, often turn against the particular hierarchies that made the Lowell name seem "significant, illustrative, American, etc." When a patrician name like it enters a contemporary poem, it is more likely to arouse bewilderment or derision than concern for a great family's legacy. "No one, much less / my parents, can tell me why / / my middle name is Lowell," Kevin Young writes, not pursuing the matter any further.

Instead, contemporary poets often focus on a different task. "I know history," Richard Silken declares, "There are many names in history / / but none of them are ours." Sharing his sense of outrage, contemporary poets have taken the challenge of adding "our" "names" to the public record, presenting a new account of American history and culture.

In some cases, the introduction of these names helps poets to assert their historical claims and self-definitions. In her collection, Postcolonial Love Poem, winner of the 2021 Pulitzer Prize in Poetry, Natalie Diaz, Mojave and an enrolled member of the Gila River Indian Tribe, describes the Colorado River as "My river" and remembers it before it was "shattered by fifteen dams." To addresses this damage, the poem restores the landscape and its inhabitants to their native names, "'Achii 'ahan, Mojave salmon, / Colorado pikeminnow" and "Achii 'ahan nyuunye— / our words for *Milky Way*." Referring to "our words," Diaz's bilingualism insists on the primacy of the native expression. When Diaz states her tribal name, she stresses its essential truth. "'Aha Makav' is not simply a word—an arbitrary connection between a sound and meaning, as some linguists would say—but a God-given expression of the intimate connection between Creator, land, and humanity," "'Aha Makav' is the true name of our people, given to us by our Creator who / loosed the river from the earth and built it into our living bodies." Of course such spiritual claims also carry a political charge, as when Diaz exposes the history that certain names conceal once their origins are overlooked, if not forgotten. "Manhattan is a Lenape word," she pointedly reminds her readers.

More commonly, the poets add the names of people, not places. The title poem of Jericho Brown's *The Tradition*, the winner of the 2020 Pulitzer Prize in poetry, portrays African American men gardening: "*Aster. Nasturtium. Delphinium.* We thought / Fingers in dirt meant it was our dirt" "in elements classical / Philosophers said could change us." As the poem describes "men like me and my brothers" playing at high speed a recording of the flowers they planted, "proof we existed," the poem speeds to a shocking end, describing "colors you expect in poems / Where the world ends, everything cut down. / *John Crawford. Eric Garner. Mike Brown.*" The list of these African American men killed by the police

10. Natalie Diaz reads at the Returning the Gift Festival in Milwaukee, Wisconsin, in 2012. "Because I write primarily in the English language," she observes, "it always feels dangerous to me—that I must work against English even as I'm writing in it."

explains why the others rush to establish "proof we existed." They fear that they too may be "cut down" at any moment.

The concluding couplet's rhyme clinches the point, rhyming the name that the poet shares with one of the killed men, "Brown": "Where the world ends, everything cut down. / *John Crawford. Eric Garner. Mike Brown.*" If these names were arranged in a different order, that effect would be lessened, if not lost. The rhyme's emphasis on "Brown" underscores the poet's connection with the dead. Subtly, it evokes his fear that his own name might soon join their list.

The sonnet form intensifies the poem's contradictory effects. "I feel completely in love with and oppressed by the sonnet," Brown has observed and this ambivalence ripples through "The Tradition." While Renaissance sonneteers boasted of their power to confer immortality, Brown expresses a more embattled hope. No poem can stop the destruction he witnesses. Unable to halt it, the final line simply lists the latest victims: "*John Crawford. Eric Garner. Mike Brown.*" The sonnet's brevity will not let the poet linger, but the form's long history and well-established strategies help him to memorialize Crawford, Garner, and Brown. Each name fills a sentence; together, they comprise the poem's final line. By doing so, Brown bestows a certain dignity to the dead, honoring them in Western culture's most enduring verse form, making the list of their names into a solemn memorial.

The names that end Brown's poem have become canonical in contemporary American poetry. Seen as "significant, illustrative, American, etc.," they inspire some of the present moment's most admired poems. These poems vary in style, structure, and argument. Ranging in their approaches, they share the determination that America's poetic and cultural history not only acknowledge these names but also, more important, honor them.

In "A Small Needful Fact," Ross Gay builds a poem from an ostensibly minor detail he learned from the obituary of one of the men whom Jericho Brown mentions. Continuing the sentence that the title starts, "A Small Needful Fact," the poem opens, "Is that Eric Garner worked / for some time for the Parks and Rec. / Horticultural Department." The one-sentence poem proceeds through a series of qualifications, noting that "perhaps, in all likelihood, / he put gently into the earth / some plants" and "some of them, in all likelihood, / continue to grow" before revising Garner's famous plea for his life, "I can't breathe," into a celebration of his legacy, speculating that some of the plants Garner planted continue "making it easier / for us to breathe."

"A Small Needful Fact" restores a sense of Garner's life beyond the awful images that bystanders filmed on their cell phones. Tellingly, Gay places Garner in a bucolic setting, not the Staten Island sidewalk where the police violently arrested him for selling untaxed cigarettes. Like Brown, Gay writes pastoral poetry, but Gay celebrates nature more enthusiastically, praising its crucial, life-sustaining qualities:

> what such plants do, like house
> and feed small and necessary creatures,
> like being pleasant to touch and smell

These images of the shelter and sustenance that nature provides are especially striking, given African American poetry's complicated relation to that subject. As Camille Dungy has noted, African American poetry about nature tends to "defy the pastoral conventions of Western poetry." "The traditional context of the nature poem in the Western intellectual tradition," Dungy observes, "informs the prevailing views of the natural world as a place of positive collaboration, refuge, idyllic rural life, or wilderness." In contrast, African American poetry often views nature from "the perspective of the workers of the field," emphasizing the labor, forced or voluntary, and the violence that takes place there, not serene relaxation and rejuvenation.

In "A Small Needful Fact," Gay combines both kinds of pastoral. He presents Garner as a "worker of the field," an employee of the "Parks and Rec. / Horticultural Department," and nature "as a place of positive collaboration" and a "refuge" for insects and humans alike. In this respect, "A Small Needful Fact" resembles the plants Gay describes: a tender counterforce to the suffering the world inflicts.

In contrast to Gay's quiet poem, Danez Smith's consideration of the same death boils with frustrated anger. Smith rails against the need for the kind of poem he writes, mourning another African American killed by the police. "I am sick of writing this poem," the poem opens, intriguingly titled "not an elegy for Mike Brown." In an interview, Smith, who is genderqueer and uses plural pronouns, explains the distinction they draw between their poem and an elegy: "To only know a person because of their death is something different to being able to really celebrate the life, which is what I think an elegy should be able to do.... But I didn't actually know the texture of these people's living, so I was only able to love someone because of their victimhood. So 'not an elegy' allows a respectful distance." Smith writes what literary scholars classify as a public elegy, not a personal one, mourning someone they did not know but whose death illuminates the cultural moment.

Accordingly, Smith treats Brown as a public figure, not a private one. Unlike Gay imagining Eric Garner "put[ing] gently into the earth / some plants," Smith presents Brown in canonical terms, likening him to Helen of Troy. "think: once, a white girl / / was kidnapped & that's the Trojan war," he observes. "I demand a war to bring the dead boy back / no matter what his name is this time."

The forcefulness of Smith's "demand" testifies to the powerlessness that fuels it. The poet does not command an army. Even if they did, though, no army could "bring the dead boy back." The poem resents its necessity; it rages against another death of another African American killed by police, another stranger the poet is "able to love…because of their victimhood." Smith wants to "celebrate life," but must settle for another kind of mourning. As with many other poems about the untimely deaths of African Americans, the poem bitterly turns against its occasion. "This should not be the brick and mortar / of poetry," as Reginald Dwayne Betts puts it in "When I Think of Tamir Rice while Driving," "the moment when a black father drives / his black sons to school & the thing in the air is the death / of a black boy that the father cannot mention."

In "Domestic Violence," Roger Reeves summons ancestral, poetic, and divine powers to mitigate this powerlessness. The poem describes Louis Till, Emmett Till's father, touring the afterlife. As a private in the US Army, Louis Till was incarcerated with Ezra Pound at Pisa. Convicted during a military trial whose verdict has been questioned, Till was executed for rape and murder. "Till was hung yesterday / for murder and rape with trimmings," Pound wrote in *The Cantos*. In "Domestic Violence," Till encounters Pound but flees from his intrusive influence: "I ran from Ezra who ran after me and demanded he be / My guide." He also has a rather lackluster meeting with T. S. Eliot, who "said nothing and ran on / Into the darkness." Instead of Pound or Eliot, Till follows a chorus of African American women poets, "Audre, Gwendolyn, / And Lucille," that is, Audre Lorde, Gwendolyn Brooks, and Lucille Clifton, as "they walked on the edge of the abyss."

Like Brown's "The Tradition," "Domestic Violence" ends with a list of the names of African American victims of white violence. Reeves's furious burst of names enlarges Brown's. It includes famous and less well-known figures, intoned by the African river goddess Oya, traditionally the righter of injustice and the conduit between the living and the dead:

Eric Garner Emmett Till Freddie Gray
Korryn Gaines Trayvon Martin Martin Luther
King Jr. El-Hajj Malik El-Shabazz Fred Hampton
Kalief Browder Sandra Bland Rumain Brisbon
Akai Gurley Tamir Rice Laquan McDonald
Kajieme Powell Ezell Ford Dante Parker
Michael Brown John Crawford III Tyree Woodson
Victor White III Yvettte Smith McKenzie Cochran
Jordan Baker Andy Lopez Miriam
Carey Jonathan Ferrell Carlos Alcis
Larry Jackson Jr. Kimani Gray Rekia Boyd
Malissa Williams Timothy Russell
Reynaldo Cuevas Chavis Carter Shantel Davis
Henry Dumas Sharmel Edwards Shereese Francis
Wendell Allen Deion Fludd. Flood. Flood.

The literary power of these lines arises from their cumulative effect, the repetition of example after example, an evocation of the magnitude of the loss. The list insists that all the names it includes are "historic," of great and enduring importance. It memorializes, laments, and, rather extraordinarily, affirms. As the poem describes it, to say the names is to release the dead from their suffering. "The gates of the cemetery / Are now open," the goddess concludes and Louis Till watches the effect that the "Flood" of the victims' names achieves, "A great tumult started: / Water, the clanging of machetes, and the boy, / / My namesake, heading up into the limbs of a tree."

To arrive at the moment of healing and ascension, Reeves, like Till, travels past Pound and Eliot, noticing them but finding assistance elsewhere. His timely poetry shows how persistently the two main characteristics of American poetry continue to inspire poets, even those skeptical about many of America's literary traditions. Whether in Brown's sonnet, Gay's pastoralism, Smith's analogy of the Trojan War, or the purgatorial journey that

Reeves starts with an epigraph from Dante, each poet approaches the distinctively American version of racial violence with techniques and conventions that originate from outside the country's borders. As in the case of the sonnet and the pastoral, the poets draw from these traditions ambivalently, "completely in love with and oppressed by" them (as Brown observed).

These poems follow contemporary American poetry's foundational collection, Claudia Rankine's *Citizen: An American Lyric*. To memorialize African Americans recently killed by racial violence, Rankine presents each name in the same form. The list proceeds chronologically by the date of the deaths, starting "In Memory of Jordan Russell David," the Florida teen shot by a middle-aged white man after he and his friends refused to turn down the music in their car, and ending "In Memory of Jamar Clark," the twenty-four-year-old shot by a Minneapolis policeman. Nine of the twenty were murdered in the Emmanuel AME Church in Charleston, South Carolina, when a white gunman shot the worshipers after joining their Bible study session; nine also were killed by police or died in police custody. Their names span ages and distances. Tamir Rice, the youngest victim, was twelve years old when he was killed; Susie Jackson, the oldest, was eighty-seven. Underscoring racial violence's vastness, the violence they suffered took place in states as different as Florida, Ohio, Maryland, Texas, Illinois, South Carolina, and New York.

After the last name, the text hauntingly repeats "In Memory" eight times, with the words fading until they cannot be seen. The repetitions of "In Memory" await more names for the reason that the next page explains with epigrammatic concision, "Because white men can't / police their imagination / black men are dying." The haiku commands an entire page, and the blank space that surrounds it reinforces the stark truth. Confirming it, a subsequent edition added four names: Alton Sterling, Philando

Castile, Jordan Edwards, and Stephon Clark, all African American men shot and killed by the police.

Citizen: An American Lyric contributes to American poetry a recognition of racial violence's ordinariness, that the deaths the poems memorialize should not be regarded as isolated or exceptional events. Rather, they exist on a continuum with the daily slights that many African Americans frequently endure. Together the poems dramatize the psychological burdens that racism places on African Americans, whether a celebrity such as Serena Williams (the subject of one section) or the anonymous figures of other poems. As part of her research, Rankine interviewed friends and the poems explore the experiences they shared. In this sense, the poems are less autographical than social and collective.

To dramatize the moments' accumulative force, the poems often emphasize the casualness of the insults. When a stranger insults some teenagers with the English language's most offensive word, he does so in America's blandly popular social space: "When the stranger asks, Why do you care? you just stand there staring at him. He has just referred to the boisterous teenagers in Starbucks as niggers. Hey, I am standing right here, you responded, not necessarily expecting him to turn to you."

Tellingly, the poem begins with the stranger's challenge, "Why do you care?" as if the speaker had violated social decorum, not him. He remains unembarrassed, let alone apologetic. Even the speaker's objection, "Hey, I am standing right here," qualifies the outrage it expresses. The speaker, presumably the only African American nearby, instinctively protests the stranger insulting the teenagers in their presence. By implication, the speaker accepts that whites still use the slur when African Americans cannot hear them. The speaker miscalculates, assuming the fact they overheard the expletive will cause the man to recognize a very modest point: that he should not use the racial slur in the presence of an African American.

As the subtitle indicates, Rankine writes what she calls *An American Lyric*. Several techniques contribute to this effort. Composed largely in prose paragraphs, the collection is not easy to classify, a fact the National Book Critics Circle acknowledged when it bestowed a rare honor on *Citizen: An American Lyric*, naming it as a finalist in two different categories: in poetry (which it won) and in criticism. Many of the poems in *Citizen* also employ the second person. They address the reader as if the reader were also the speaker. Autobiographical poetry typically favors the first person, which encourages readers to associate the speaker with a dramatized version of the poet. In contrast, *Citizen: An American Lyric* retains a certain anonymity. Just as the unnamed speaker shifts from poem to poem, the second-person address complicates the reader's experience of the poem, urging the reader to consider how fully this situation applies to them, if the reader faces the same stresses and erasures or experiences the same spaces differently. For example, the speaker's objection, "Hey, I am standing right here," would convey a different meaning if said by a white speaker. Filled with such moments, the poems return to the question of how our racial identities inform our daily interactions and how racism fractures the notion of a shared citizenship.

Writing in 1951, W. H. Auden described how the greatest artists of the twentieth century, "the innovators, the creators of the new style," witnessed the birth of a new epoch, modernism. "Radical changes and significant novelty in artistic style can only occur when there has been a radical change in human sensibility to require them," Auden observed. "Before a similar crop of revolutionary artists can appear again, there will have to be just such another cultural revolution replacing these attitudes with others." A hundred years after modernism's great burst of artistic innovation and radical change, this introduction to American poetry ends during another disorienting time, a summer of coronavirus, Black Lives Matter protests, economic uncertainty, and the bewildering disorders of the Trump presidency.

Judgments of the present are notoriously unreliable and predictions even worse. Many poets promoting contemporary social justice movements urge a "cultural revolution," and if in fact we are witnessing one, their poetry may very well clarify the radical change in human sensibility we are undergoing, its necessity and limitations, and the innovations it will bestow to our country and its art.

References

Chapter 1: American poetry's two characteristics

Walt Whitman, "Letter to Ralph Waldo Emerson," August 1856, Walt
　Whitman Archive.

T. S. Eliot, "Reflections on Contemporary Poetry," *The Egoist*
　(September 1917): 118.

Anne Bradstreet, *The Works of Anne Bradstreet*, ed. Jeannine Hensley
　(Cambridge, MA: Harvard University Press, 1967), 79.

Bradstreet, *Works of Anne Bradstreet*, 184.

Massachusetts Bay Company, *The Puritans' Farewell to England*,
　facsimile ed. (New York: The Society, 1912), 4–5.

William Bradford, *Of Plymouth Plantation, 1620–1647*, ed. Samuel
　Eliot Morison (New York: Knopf, 2002), 302.

Bradstreet, *Works of Anne Bradstreet*, 187, 179.

Charlotte Gordon, *Mistress Bradstreet: The Untold Life of America's
　First Poet* (New York: Little, Brown, 2005), 208–9; and Emory
　Elliott, "New England Puritan Literature: Poetry," in *The
　Cambridge History of American Literature*, ed. Sacvan Bercovitch,
　vol. 1, *1590–1820* (Cambridge: Cambridge University Press,
　1994), 239.

Wallace Stevens, *The Collected Poems* (New York: Vintage, 1991), 160.

"Common Grackle," Cornell Lab of Ornithology: All About Birds.
　https://www.allaboutbirds.org/guide/Common_Grackle/sounds.

Diane J. Rayor, trans., *Sappho: A New Translation of the Complete
　Works* (New York: Cambridge University Press, 2014), 76.

Percy Bysshe Shelley, "A Defence of Poetry," in *Literary Criticism: Pope
　to Croce*, ed. Gay Wilson Allen and Harry Hayden Clark (Detroit:
　Wayne State University Press, 1962), 306.

Wallace Stevens, *Opus Posthumous*, ed. Milton J. Bates (New York: Vintage, 1989), 259, 260, 212.

Stevens, *Collected Poems*, 131.

Wallace Stevens, *The Necessary Angel: Essays on Reality and the Imagination* (New York: Knopf, 1951), 36.

Stevens, *Collected Poems*, 160.

Langston Hughes, *The Big Sea* (New York: Hill & Wang, 1998), 54.

Langston Hughes, *The Collected Poems of Langston Hughes*, ed. Arnold Rampersad (New York: Vintage, 1994), 23.

Rachel Blau DuPlessis, *Genders, Races, and Religious Cultures in Modern American Poetries, 1908–1934* (Cambridge: Cambridge University Press, 2001), 95.

Hughes, *Collected Poems*, 24.

T. S. Eliot, "American Literature and the American Language," *The Sewanee Review* 74, no. 1 (Winter 1966): 13.

Eric Foner, *The Fiery Trial: Abraham Lincoln and American Slavery* (New York: Norton, 2011), 8, 10.

Hughes, *The Big Sea*, 55.

Faith Berry, *Langston Hughes, before and beyond Harlem* (New York: Citadel Press, 1992), 161.

Hughes, *Collected Poems*, 162.

Arnold Rampersad, *The Life of Langston Hughes*, vol. 1, *1902–1941, I, Too, Sing America* (New York: Oxford University Press, 2002), 252. See also 242–75, which details Hughes's trip to the Soviet Union.

Hughes, *Collected Poems*, 166.

Arnold Rampersad, *Life of Langston Hughes*, 390. See also Rampersad's note on the poem in Hughes, *Collected Poems*, 642.

Fred Jerome and Rodger Taylor, *Einstein on Race and Racism* (New Brunswick, NJ: Rutgers University Press, 2006), 170.

Executive Sessions of the Senate Permanent Subcommittee on Investigations of the Committee on Government Operations, Vol. 2, Eighty-Third Congress First Session, 1953, made public January 2003, https://www.govinfo.gov/content/pkg/CPRT-107SPRT83870/html/CPRT-107SPRT83870.htm.

Jonathan Flatley, "Beaten, but Unbeatable: On Langston Hughes's Black Feminism," in *Comintern Aesthetics*, ed. Amelia M. Glaser and Steven S. Lee (Toronto: University of Toronto Press, 2020), 333.

Elizabeth Bishop, *Poems* (New York: Farrar, Straus and Giroux, 2011), 198, 122.

Elizabeth Bishop, *The Collected Prose*, ed. Robert Giroux (New York: Farrar, Straus and Giroux, 1984), 26. Bishop's allergic reaction is detailed in Brett C. Millier, *Elizabeth Bishop: Life and the Memory of It* (Berkeley: University of California Press, 1992), 244–45.

Bishop, *Poems*, 91–92.

Chapter 2: American English as a poetic resource

Harryette Mullen, *Sleeping with the Dictionary* (Berkeley: University of California Press, 2002), 67.

Mullen, *Sleeping with the Dictionary*, 67.

Harryette Mullen, *The Cracks between What We Are and What We Are Supposed to Be: Essays and Interviews* (Tuscaloosa: University of Alabama Press, 2012), 209.

Barbara Henning, "Conversation with Harryette Mullen: From B to D," *Eoagh*, https://eoagh.com/conversation-with-harryette-mullen-from-b-to-d/.

Mullen, *Sleeping with the Dictionary*, 19.

Stephanie Burt, *Close Calls with Nonsense: Reading New Poetry* (St. Paul, MN: Graywolf, 2009), 13; and Margo Natalie Crawford, "What Was Is: The Time and Space of Entanglement Erased by Post-Blackness," in *The Trouble with Post-Blackness*, ed. Houston A. Baker and K. Merinda Simmons (New York: Columbia University Press, 2015), 32.

Mullen, *Cracks Between*, 47; and Mullen, *Sleeping with the Dictionary*, 67.

Christopher Hennessy, "An Interview with John Ashbery," in *Our Deep Gossip: Conversations with Gay Writers on Poetry and Desire* (Madison: University of Wisconsin Press, 2013), 58.

Juan Felipe Herrera, *Notes on the Assemblage* (San Francisco: City Lights, 2015), 59.

Joy Harjo, *When the Light of the World Was Subdued, Our Songs Came Through: A Norton Anthology of Native Nations Poetry* (New York: Norton, 2020), 2.

Homi Bhabha, *The Location of Culture* (London: Routledge, 1994), 59.

Walt Whitman, *The Neglected Walt Whitman: Vital Texts*, ed. Sam Abrams (New York: Four Walls Books, 1993), 158.

Walt Whitman, *Walt Whitman: Poetry and Prose* (New York: Library of America, 1982), 51.

Kenneth M. Price, *Walt Whitman: The Contemporary Reviews* (Cambridge: Cambridge University Press, 1996), 96; and anonymous review of *Leaves of Grass*, *The National Quarterly Review*, September 2, 1860, 515–17. https://whitmanarchive.org/criticism/reviews/lg1860/anc.00243.html.

Ralph Waldo Emerson, *The Collected Works of Ralph Waldo Emerson*, vol. 2, *Essays*, second series, ed. Alfred Riggs Ferguson, Joseph Slater, and Jean Ferguson Carr (Cambridge, MA: Harvard University Press, 1983), 21, 22.

John Townsend Trowbridge, *My Own Story: With Recollection of Noted Persons* (Boston: Houghton Mifflin, 1903), 367.

Walt Whitman [unsigned in original], "Walt Whitman and His Poems," *The United States Review* 5 (September 1855): 205–12. https://whitmanarchive.org/criticism/reviews/lg1860/anc.00044.html.

Whitman, *Poetry and Prose*, 5.

Ted Genoways made this rather startling discovery. See his essay, "'One Goodshaped and Wellhung Man': Accentuated Sexuality and the Uncertain Authorship of the Frontispiece to the 1855 Edition of *Leaves of Grass*," in *Leaves of Grass: The Sesquicentennial Essays*, ed. Susan Belasco, Ed Folsom, and Kenneth M. Price (Lincoln: University of Nebraska Press, 2007), 88–123.

Whitman, *Poetry and Prose*, 27, 50.

Quoted in David S. Reynolds, *Walt Whitman's America: A Cultural Biography* (New York: Vintage Books, 1996), 244. My discussion of von Humboldt's influence on Whitman draws from Reynolds's account.

Walt Whitman, *The Collected Writings of Walt Whitman*, vol. 3, ed. William White (New York: New York University Press, 1978), 669.

Whitman, *Poetry and Prose*, 87.

Whitman, *Poetry and Prose*, 41.

Whitman, *Poetry and Prose*, 85.

Whitman, *Poetry and Prose*, 93.

Whitman, *Poetry and Prose*, 6.

Whitman, *Poetry and Prose*, 5–6.

Henry Wadsworth Longfellow, *The Works of Henry Wadsworth Longfellow*, vol. 2, ed. Samuel Longfellow (Boston: Houghton, Mifflin, 1891), 20.

Henry Wadsworth Longfellow, *Poems and Other Writings*, ed. J. D. McClatchy (New York: Library of America, 2000), 754–55.

Longfellow, *Poems and Other Writings*, 141.

Longfellow, *Poems and Other Writings*, 336.

Longfellow, *Poems and Other Writings*, 335.

Walt Whitman, *Complete Poetry and Collected Prose*, 50.

Ed Folsom, "Introduction," in *Walt Whitman: The Measure of His Song*, ed. Jim Perlman and Ed Folsom (Duluth, MN: Holy Cow! Press, 1998), 22, which also quotes Harvey.

June Jordan, "For the Sake of People's Poetry: Walt Whitman and the Rest of Us," Poetry Foundation, August 15, 2006, https://www.poetryfoundation.org/articles/68627/for-the-sake-of-peoples-poetry.

Jorge Luis Borges and Kirsten Dehner, "Jorge Luis Borges on 'Leaves of Grass,'" *Columbia: A Journal of Literature and Art* no. 8 (Spring/Summer 1983): 10, 13.

Fernando Pessoa, *Poems of Fernando Pessoa*, trans. Edwin Honig and Susan M. Brown (San Francisco: City Light Books, 1986), 82; and Federico García Lorca, "Ode to Walt Whitman," trans. Ben Belitt, *Poetry* 85, no. 4 (January 1955): 191.

Ashley Davidson, "My Barbaric Yawp: Luis Alberto Ambroggio on translating Walt Whitman," Shambaugh House, February 24, 2014, https://iwp.uiowa.edu/shse/2014-02-24/my-barbaric-yawp-luis-alberto-ambroggio-on-translating-walt-whitman; and Luis Alberto Ambroggio, *Todos somos Whitman/We Are All Whitman*, English and Spanish ed., trans. Brett Alan Sanders (Houston: Arte Publico Press, 2016).

Lawrence Buell, "Introduction," in *Selected Poems*, ed. Henry Wadsworth Longfellow, Kindle ed. (New York: Penguin Books, 1988).

Longfellow, *Poems and Other Writings*, 337.

Dwight Garner, "Louise Glück, a Nobel Laureate Whose Poems Have Abundant Intellect and Deep Feeling," *New York Times*, October 10, 2020, C1.

Edgar Allan Poe, *Essays and Reviews*, ed. Gary Richard Thompson (New York: Library of America, 1984), 763.

Ezra Pound, *Literary Essays of Ezra Pound*, ed. T. S Eliot (New York: New Directions, 1968), 34.

Ezra Pound, "What I Feel about Walt Whitman," in *Walt Whitman: The Measure of His Song*, ed. Jim Perlman and Ed Folsom (Duluth, MN: Holy Cow! Press, 1998), 112.

Ezra Pound, *Selected Poems of Ezra Pound* (New York: New Directions, 1957), 27.

Pound, *Literary Essays*, 3.

Ezra Pound, *The Pisan Cantos*, ed. Richard Sieburth (New York: New Directions, 2003), 96.

Pound, *Pisan Cantos*, 49.

Pound, *Pisan Cantos*, 99.

Pound, *Pisan Cantos*, 61.

William Carlos Williams, "Letter to Harold Norse," August 26, 1960, in *The Outlaw Bible of American Poetry*, ed. Alan Kaufman (New York: Basic Books, 1999), 159.

William Carlos Williams, *Paterson*, rev. ed. (New York: New Directions, 1992), 222.

William Carlos Williams, *Selected Poems*, ed. Charles Tomlinson (New York: New Directions, 1976), 74.

William Carlos Williams, *Selected Essays of William Carlos Williams* (New York: New Directions, 1969), 177.

Ezra Pound, *The Selected Letters of Ezra Pound, 1907–1941*, ed. D. D. Paige (New York: New Directions, 1971), 123–24, 322.

William Carlos Williams, *The William Carlos Williams Reader*, ed. M. L. Rosenthal (New York: New Directions, 1965), 21.

Williams, *Selected Poems*, 262.

Williams, *William Carlos Williams Reader*, 380.

Robert Frost, *The Poetry of Robert Frost: The Collected Poems*, ed. Edward Connery Lathem (New York: Henry Holt, 1982), 52.

Robert Frost, *The Robert Frost Reader: Poetry and Prose*, ed. Edward Connery Lathem and Lawrance Thompson (New York: Henry Holt, 1972), 284.

Frost, *Robert Frost Reader*, 462.

Frost, *Poetry of Robert Frost*, 52.

Frost, *Robert Frost Reader*, 462.

Laurence Buell, "Frost as a New England Poet," in *The Cambridge Companion to Robert Frost*, ed. Robert Faggen (Cambridge: Cambridge University Press, 2001), 102.

Frost, *Poetry of Robert Frost*, 119, 120.

Rae Armantrout, interview with Matt Raymond, 2010 National Book Festival, Library of Congress.

Rae Armantrout, *Just Saying* (Middletown, CT: Wesleyan Press, 2013), 45.

Naomi Shihab Nye, *You and Yours* (Rochester, NY: BOA Editions, 2005), 51.

Solmaz Sharif, *Look* (Minneapolis, MN: Graywolf, 2016), 55.

Williams, *Selected Essays*, 172.

Chapter 3: Convention and idiosyncrasy

Phillis Wheatley, *Complete Writings*, ed. Vincent Carretta (New York: Penguin Books, 2001), 8.

Wheatley, *Complete Writings*, 7.

Wheatley, *Complete Writings*, 8.

Wheatley, *Complete Writings*, 13.

Henry Louis Gates, *The Trials of Phillis Wheatley: America's First Black Poet and Her Encounters with the Founding Fathers* (New York: Basic Civitas, 2010), 71. My account of Wheatley's trial also relies on Gates's account.

Wheatley, *Complete Writings*, 40.

Thomas Jefferson, "Notes on the State of Virginia," in *The Writings of Thomas Jefferson*, vol. 2, Electronic Text Center, University of Virginia Library. https://web.archive.org/web/20110221130550/http://etext.lib.virginia.edu/etcbin/toccer-new2?id=JefVirg.sgm&images=images/modeng&data=/texts/english/modeng/parsed&tag=public&part=all.

Quoted in Eric Ashley Hairston, *The Ebony Column: Classics, Civilization, and the African American Reclamation of the West* (Knoxville: University of Tennessee Press, 2013), 37.

J. Paul Hunter, "Couplets and Conversation," in *The Cambridge Companion to Eighteenth-Century Poetry*, ed. John Sitter (Cambridge: Cambridge University Press, 2001), 21.

Alexander Pope, *The Major Works* (Oxford: Oxford University Press, 2006), 29; and Wheatley, *Complete Writings*, 9.

Amiri Baraka, *The LeRoi Jones/Amiri Baraka Reader*, ed. William J. Harris (New York: Basic Books, 1999), 313.

Ezra Pound, *Make It New: Essays* (New Haven, CT: Yale University Press, 1935); and Williams, *Selected Essays*, 21.

Emily Dickinson, *The Letters of Emily Dickinson*, ed. Thomas H. Johnson (Cambridge, MA: Harvard University Press, 1986), 94.

Willis J. Buckingham, *Emily Dickinson's Reception in the 1890s: A Documentary History* (Pittsburgh, PA: University of Pittsburgh Press, 1989), 176.

Buckingham, *Emily Dickinson's Reception*, 8.

Emily Dickinson, *The Collected Poems* (Philadelphia: Courage Books, 1991), 94.

Emily Dickinson, *Poems*, ed. Mabel Loomis Todd and T. W. Higginson (Boston: Roberts Brothers, 1893), v.

Buckingham, *Emily Dickinson's Reception*, xv.

Emily Dickinson, *The Complete Poems of Emily Dickinson*, ed. Thomas H. Johnson (Boston: Little, Brown, 1960), 118; and Emily Dickinson, *Collected Poems*, 65.

Buckingham, *Emily Dickinson's Reception*, xvii.

Emily Dickinson, *Selected Letters*, ed. Thomas H. Johnson (Cambridge, MA: Harvard University Press, 1986), 225, 231.

Jed Deppman, *Trying to Think with Emily Dickinson* (Amherst: University of Massachusetts Press, 2008), 110.

Dickinson, *Complete Poems*, 254, 744.

Dickinson, *Complete Poems*, 794.

Dickinson, *Complete Poems*, 460, 450.

Dickinson, *Complete Poems*, 143.

Dickinson, *Complete Poems*, 247.

Buckingham, *Emily Dickinson's Reception*, 54.

Noah Webster and Chauncey A. Goodridge, *An American Dictionary of the English Language* (Springfield, MA: G. and C. Merriam, 1848), 1056.

Adrienne Rich, *Adrienne Rich's Poetry and Prose*, ed. Albert Gelpi (New York: Norton, 1993), 189.

Susan Howe, *My Emily Dickinson* (New York: New Directions, 2007), 133.

Dickinson, *Selected Letters*, 172.

Howe, *My Emily Dickinson*, 11.

Alicia Suskin Ostriker, *Stealing the Language: The Emergence of Women's Poetry in America* (Boston: Beacon Press, 1987), 43.

Yvor Winters, *Primitivism and Decadence: A Study of American Experimental Poetry* (New York: Arrow Editions, 1937), 136, 49.

Donald Justice, *Oblivion: On Writers and Writing* (Ashland, OR: Story Line Press, 1998), 7–8.

Donald Justice, *New and Selected Poems* (New York: Knopf, 2009), 149.

Philip Hoy, *Anthony Hecht in Conversation with Philip Hoy* (London: Between the Lines, 1988), 24.

Rich, *Adrienne Rich's Poetry and Prose*, 171.

Rich, *Adrienne Rich's Poetry and Prose*, 278–79.

Rich, *Adrienne Rich's Poetry and Prose*, 3, 5.

Rich, *Adrienne Rich's Poetry and Prose*, 4.

Rich, *Adrienne Rich's Poetry and Prose*, 4.

Rich, *Adrienne Rich's Poetry and Prose*, 167.

Rich, *Adrienne Rich's Poetry and Prose*, 115.

Rich, *Adrienne Rich's Poetry and Prose*, 42–43.

Adrienne Rich, *Diving into the Wreck: Poems 1971–1972* (New York: Norton, 1973), dust jacket.

Charles Bernstein, *Parsing/Jäsentäen* (Norderstedt, Germany: BoD, 2009), 107.

Bernstein, *Parsing/Jäsentäen*, 107.

Charles Bernstein, *My Way: Speeches and Poems* (Chicago: University of Chicago Press, 1999), 2–3.

Ben Lerner, *The Topeka School* (New York: Farrar, Straus and Giroux, 2019), 88.

Maggie Smith, "Good Bones," *Waxwing* IX (Summer 2016), http://waxwingmag.org/items/Issue9/28_Smith-Good-Bones.php.

Pound, *Literary Essays*, 11.

Chapter 4: Auden and Eliot: Two complicating examples

Edward O'Shea, "Seamus Heaney at Berkeley, 1970–71," *Southern California Quarterly* 98, no. 2 (2016): 165.

Hugh Kenner, *A Colder Eye: The Modern Irish Writers* (New York: Knopf, 1983), 25. For a notable differing view, see Jahan Ramazani's *A Transnational Poetics* (Chicago: University of Chicago Press, 2009).

W. B. Yeats, *Selected Poems and Four Plays*, ed. M. L. Rosenthal (New York: Scribner, 1996), 153, 210.

Thom Gunn, *Collected Poems* (New York: Farrar, Straus and Giroux, 1994), 40, 489. For a thoughtful presentation of the poetry Auden wrote in America as postnational, see Nicholas Jenkins, "Writing 'Without Roots': Auden, Eliot, and Post-National Poetry," in *Something We Have That They Don't: British and American Poetic Relations since 1925*, ed. Steve Clark and Mark Ford (Iowa City: University of Iowa Press, 2004), 75–97.

T. S. Eliot, *On Poetry and Poets* (New York: Farrar, Straus and Giroux, 1957), 8.

T. S. Eliot, *To Criticize the Critic* (London: Faber and Faber, 1965), 60.

Eliot, *To Criticize the Critic*, 60.

W. H. Auden, *The Complete Works of W. H. Auden: Prose*, vol. 3, *1949–1955*, ed. Edward Mendelson (Princeton, NJ: Princeton University Press, 1988), 523.

T. S. Eliot, *The Letters of T. S. Eliot*, vol. 1, *1898–1922*, ed. Valerie Eliot and Hugh Haughton, rev. ed. (New Haven, CT: Yale University Press, 2011), 338.

Eliot, *To Criticize the Critic*, 60.

Peter Edgerly Firchow, *W. H. Auden: Contexts for Poetry* (Newark: University of Delaware Press, 2002), 169.

Evelyn Waugh, *The Tablet*, May 5, 1951, 356.

Commons Sitting, Oral Answers to Questions, "Military Service (British Service Abroad)," HC Deb, June 13, 1940, vol. 361, c1361.

Philip Larkin, *Required Reading: Miscellaneous Pieces 1955–1982* (Ann Arbor: University of Michigan Press, 1999), 123, 125.

W. H. Auden, *The Complete Works of W. H. Auden: Prose*, vol. 2, *1939–1948*, ed. Edward Mendelson (Princeton, NJ: Princeton University Press, 2002), 92.

W. H. Auden, *The Collected Poems*, ed. Edward Mendelson (New York: Vintage, 1991), 831.

W. H. Auden, *The Complete Works of W. H. Auden: Prose*, vol. 6, *1969–1973*, ed. Edward Mendelson (Princeton, NJ: Princeton University Press, 2015), 509.

W. H. Auden, *Selected Poems*, ed. Edward Mendelson (New York: Vintage International, 2007), 95.

Henry Louis Mencken, *The American Language: An Inquiry into the Development of English in the United States*, 2nd ed. (New York: Knopf, 1921), 159.

Harold Norse, *Memoirs of a Bastard Angel: A Fifty-Year Literary and Erotic Odyssey* (New York: Thunder's Mouth Press, 1989), 79, 78.

Auden, *Collected Poems*, 772, 843, 844.

Joseph Brodsky, *Less Than One: Selected Essays* (New York: Farrar, Straus and Giroux, 1986), 307. Others have judged Auden's use of American slang much more harshly. Kenneth Rexroth, for instance, attacked Auden's use of American slang as awkwardly mannered, charging, "WH. Auden has spent years in *America* and never learned to use a single phrase of *American slang* without sounding like a British music-hall Yank comic and his verse has remained as British, as specifically 'school,' as Matthew Arnold." See Kenneth Rexroth, "The Poetry of Denise Levertov," in *Denise Levertov: Selected Criticism*, ed. Albert Gelpi (Ann Arbor: University of Michigan Press, 1993), 13.

Yeats, *Selected Poems and Four Plays*, 83.

Auden, *Complete Works of W. H. Auden: Prose, 1939–1948*, 62, 63.

Auden, *Complete Works of W. H. Auden: Prose, 1939–1948*, 173.

Yeats, *Selected Poems and Four Plays*, 84.

American Poetry

Auden, *Selected Poems*, 96.

Auden, *Complete Works of W. H. Auden: Prose, 1939–1948*, 42.

W. H. Auden, *New Year Letter* (London: Faber and Faber, 1941), 53.

Yeats, *Selected Poems and Four Plays*, 84.

Auden, *Selected Poems*, 97.

Quoted in Edward Mendelson, *The Early Auden* (New York: Farrar, Straus and Giroux, 1981), 326.

Auden, *Selected Poems*, 95.

Quoted in Mendelson, *Early Auden*, 330.

Auden, *Collected Poems*, 265.

James Held, "Ironic Harmony: Blues Convention and Auden's 'Refugee Blues,'" *Journal of Modern Literature* 18, no. 1 (Winter 1992): 140.

Hughes, *Collected Poems*, 72.

Albert Murray, *Stomping the Blues* (Minneapolis: University of Minnesota Press, 2017), 118.

See Steven C. Tracy, *Langston Hughes & the Blues* (Urbana: University of Illinois Press, 2001), 156–58.

Genevieve Abravanel, *Americanizing Britain: The Rise of Modernism in the Age of the Entertainment Empire* (New York: Oxford University Press, 2012), 67.

Auden, *Collected Poems*, 729.

Auden, *Collected Poems*, 730.

Auden, *Collected Poems*, 731.

Pound, *The Selected Letters*, 40.

T. S. Eliot, *Poems of T. S. Eliot: The Annotated Texts*, vol. 1, *Collected and Uncollected Poems*, ed. Christopher Ricks and Jim McCue (Baltimore: Johns Hopkins University Press, 2015), 5.

Eliot, *Poems of T. S. Eliot*, 6.

T. S. Eliot, *The Complete Prose of T. S. Eliot: The Critical Edition: Apprentice Years, 1905–1918*, ed. Jewel Spears Brooker and Ronald Schuchard (Baltimore: Johns Hopkins University Press, 2014), 514.

William Faulkner, *Vision in Spring* (Austin: University of Texas Press, 1984), 56.

John Berryman, *The Freedom of the Poet* (New York: Farrar, Straus and Giroux, 1976), 270, 271.

Auden, *Collected Poems*, 157; Bob Dylan, "Positively Fourth Street," Warner Brothers, 1965; and Nirvana, "All Apologies," *In Utero*, DGC, 1993.

T. S. Eliot, *The Complete Prose of T. S. Eliot: The Critical Edition: Tradition and Orthodoxy, 1934–1939*, ed. Iman Javadi, Ronald Schuchard, and Jayme Stayer (Baltimore: Johns Hopkins University Press, 2017), 303.

T. S. Eliot, *The Complete Prose of T. S. Eliot: The Critical Edition: A European Society, 1947–1953*, ed. Iman Javadi and Ronald Schuchard (Baltimore: Johns Hopkins University Press, 2019), 482–83.

T. S. Eliot, *Complete Prose of T. S. Eliot: The Critical Edition: Tradition and Orthodoxy*, 304.

T. S. Eliot, *Complete Prose of T. S. Eliot: The Critical Edition: Apprentice Years*, liii.

T. S. Eliot, *The Complete Prose of T. S. Eliot: The Critical Edition: The War Years, 1940–1946*, ed. David E. Chinitz and Ronald Schuchard (Baltimore: Johns Hopkins University Press, 2017), 601, 602.

T. S. Eliot, *Inventions of the March Hare: Poems 1909–1917*, ed. Christopher Ricks (New York: Harcourt Brace, 1996), 407.

Eliot, *Poems of T. S. Eliot*, 56.

T. S. Eliot, *The Complete Prose of T. S. Eliot: The Critical Edition: The Perfect Critic, 1919–1926*, ed. Anthony Cuda and Ronald Schuchard (Baltimore: Johns Hopkins University Press, 2014), 381.

Williams Carlos Williams, *Autobiography* (New York: Random House, 1950), 174.

James Laughlin, *Remembering William Carlos Williams* (New York: New Directions, 1995), 14–15.

Eliot, *Poems of T. S. Eliot*, 55.

Geoffrey Chaucer, *The Riverside Chaucer*, ed. Larry D. Benson, 3rd ed. (Oxford: Oxford University Press, 2008), 23.

Eliot, *Poems of T. S. Eliot*, 71.

Eliot, *Poems of T. S. Eliot*, 77.

Eliot, *Complete Prose of T. S. Eliot: The Critical Edition: The Perfect Critic*, 106.

W. H. Auden, *The Dyer's Hand and Other Essays* (New York: Random House, 1988), 365–66.

Maryemma Graham and Amritjit Singh, *Conversations with Ralph Ellison* (Jackson: University Press of Mississippi, 1995), 91.

Richard Aldington, *Life for Art's Sake: A Book of Reminiscences* (New York: Viking Press, 1941), 220–21.

Auden, *Complete Works of W. H. Auden: Prose, 1969–1973*, 599.

Eliot, *Complete Prose of T. S. Eliot: The Critical Edition: Tradition and Orthodoxy*, 306.

Eliot, *Poems of T. S. Eliot*, 185.

Eliot, *Poems of T. S. Eliot*, 193.

Eliot, *Poems of T. S. Eliot*, 185–86.

Eliot, *Poems of T. S. Eliot*, 63–64.

Eliot, *Poems of T. S. Eliot*, 187.

Eliot, *Poems of T. S. Eliot*, 933, 934.

Chapter 5: On the present and future of American poetry

Elizabeth Bishop and Robert Lowell, *Words in Air: The Complete Correspondence between Elizabeth Bishop and Robert Lowell*, ed. Thomas Travisano with Saskia Hamilton (New York: Farrar, Straus and Giroux, 2008), 247.

I have drawn information about Lowell's family from Paul L. Mariani, *Lost Puritan: A Life of Robert Lowell* (New York: Norton, 1996), especially 27–30; Kay Redfield Jamison, *Robert Lowell, Setting the River on Fire: A Study of Genius, Mania, and Character* (New York: Vintage, 2018), 43–46; and Ian Hamilton, *Robert Lowell: A Biography*, Kindle ed. (New York: Random House, 1992).

Robert Lowell, *Robert Lowell, Interviews and Memoirs*, ed. Jeffrey Meyers (Ann Arbor: University of Michigan Press, 1988), 161.

Robert Lowell, *New Selected Poems*, ed. Katie Peterson (New York: Farrar, Straus and Giroux, 2017), 68.

Hamilton, *Robert Lowell*, Kindle ed.

Lowell, *New Selected Poems*, 73.

Kevin Young, *Blue Laws: Selected and Uncollected Poems, 1995–2015* (New York: Knopf, 2017), 276.

Richard Siken, *Crush* (New Haven, CT: Yale University Press, 2005), 5.

Natalie Diaz, *Postcolonial Love Poem* (Minneapolis, MN: Graywolf Press, 2020), 61–62.

Diaz, *Postcolonial Love Poem*, 46.

Diaz, *Postcolonial Love Poem*, 14.

Jericho Brown, *The Tradition* (Port Townsend, WA: Copper Canyon Press, 2019), 10.

Candace Williams, "Gutting the Sonnet: A Conversation with Jericho Brown," *The Rumpus*, April 1, 2109.

Ross Gay, "A Small Needful Fact," Split This Rock's *The Quarry: A Social Justice Poetry Database*, 2015.

Gay, "A Small Needful Fact."

Camille Dungy, *Black Nature: Four Centuries of African American Nature Poetry* (Athens, GA: University of Georgia Press, 2009), xxi. See also xxii–xxiii.

Sandeep Parmar, "Interview with Danez Smith," *The White Review* 22 (June 2018). https://www.thewhitereview.org/feature/interview-danez-smith/.

Danez Smith, "not an elegy for Mike Brown," Split This Rock's *The Quarry: A Social Justice Poetry Database*, 2014.

Reginald Dwayne Betts, "When I Think of Tamir Rice while Driving," *Poetry* (April 2016), https://www.poetryfoundation.org/poetry magazine/poems/88739/when-i-think-of-tamir-rice-while-driving.

Pound, *Pisan Cantos*, 8.

Roger Reeves, "*Domestic Violence, Poetry*" (June 2017), https://www.poetryfoundation.org/poetrymagazine/poems/141964/domestic-violence-590c9417b5983.

Roger Reeves, "Domestic Violence." For information on "Oya," see Alexis Brooks de Vita, "Oya," *Encyclopedia of the African Diaspora* (Oxford: ABC–CLIO, 2008), 734.

Reeves, "Domestic Violence."

Claudia Rankine, *Citizen: An American Lyric* (Minneapolis, MN: Graywolf, 2014), 134; NBC News, "Florida Man Pleads Not Guilty to Shooting Teen to Death over Loud Music," November 28, 2012, http://usnews.nbcnews.com/_news/2012/11/28/15513847-florida-man-pleads-not-guilty-to-shooting-teen-to-death-over-loud-music?lite; and MPR News, "Jamar Clark Shooting, One Year Later," June 2016, https://live.mprnews.org/Event/Black_Lives_Matter_protests_in_Minneapolis_Fourth_Precinct?Page=24.

Rankine, *Citizen*, 135.

Rankine, *Citizen*, 16.

W. H. Auden, "Foreword," in Adrienne Rich, *A Change of World* (New York: Norton, 2016), xiii.

Further reading

The web offers poetry readers some very helpful resources. Both the
Academy of American Poets website (poets.org) and the Poetry
Foundation website (https://www.poetryfoundation.org) include
generous selections of poets and poetry, as well as interviews and
news items. The Emily Dickinson Archive (https://www.
edickinson.org/) presents images of Dickinson's poems in
her handwritten manuscripts. The Walt Whitman archive
(https://whitmanarchive.org/) features copious materials on
Whitman, including a variorum edition *of Leaves of Grass* (1855
edition), images of his handwritten notes and manuscripts,
contemporary reviews of Whitman's work, and multiple printed
versions of *Leaves of Grass*.

American poets have written brilliantly about their art: most notably,
Walt Whitman's "Preface" to the 1855 edition of *Leaves of Grass*
(available at the Whitman archive and in any edition of the 1855
version); Ralph Waldo Emerson's "The Poet," in The Essential
Writings of Ralph Waldo Emerson, ed. Brooks Atkinson (New
York: Modern Library, 2000), 287–305; Emily Dickinson's letters,
especially the August 1870 letter to Thomas Wentworth Higginson,
where she defined poetry by its effect, "If I feel physically as if the
top of my head were taken off, I know that is poetry," in Emily
Dickinson, *Selected Letters*, ed. Thomas H. Johnson (Cambridge,
MA: Belknap Press of Harvard University Press, 1986), 207–9;
T. S. Eliot's "Tradition and the Individual Talent" (available on the
Poetry Foundation website); Ezra Pound's "A Retrospect" and "A
Few Don'ts" (available on the Poetry Foundation website);
Langston Hughes's "The Negro Artist and the Racial Mountain"

(available on the Poetry Foundation website); and Claudia Rankine and Beth Loffreda's "Introduction" to *The Racial Imaginary: Writers on Race in the Life of the Mind* (New York: Fence, 2015).

Paul Fussell's *Poetic Meter and Poetic Form* (New York: McGraw-Hill, 1979) presents a highly readable albeit a little cranky introduction to these subjects, while James Longenbach's similarly readable but more good-natured book, *How Poems Get Made* (New York: Norton, 2019), analyzes the creative possibilities of poetry's formal elements. Jahan Ramazini's *A Transnational Poetics* (Chicago: University of Chicago, 2000) argues for modern and contemporary poetry's transnationalism.

Richard Sieburth's edition of *The Pisan Cantos* (New York: New Directions, 2003) helpfully annotates the challenging poem. Hugh Kenner's *The Pound Era* (Berkeley: University of California Press, 1973) is a brilliant, monumental work of scholarship. Dana Gioia's essay, "Longfellow in the Aftermath of Modernism," in *The Columbia History of American Poetry*, ed. Jay Parini and Brett Candlish Millier (New York: Columbia University Press, 1993), 64–96, thoughtfully reconsiders the fluctuations of Longfellow's reputation and the reasons for it. As previously mentioned, the online Walt Whitman archive (https://whitmanarchive.org/) offers a wealth of documents by and about Whitman. Unfortunately, unlike the other poets discussed in this book, Anne Bradstreet lacks a reliable, up-to-date contemporary edition.

June Jordan's "The Difficult Miracle of Black Poetry in America or Something Like a Sonnet for Phillis Wheatley," *The Massachusetts Review* 27, no. 2 (Summer 1986): 252–62, offers an important consideration of Wheatley's poetry. As its title suggests, *Adrienne Rich: Poetry and Prose*, ed. Barbara Charlesworth Gelpi, Albert Gelpi, and Brett C. Millier (New York: Norton, 2018), offers selections of Rich's poetry and prose, as well as reviews, introductions to, and scholarly essays on her work. Charles Bernstein's *Attack of the Difficult Poems: Essays and Inventions* (Chicago: University of Chicago Press, 2011) and Marjorie Perloff's *Poetry On & Off the Page: Essays for Emergent Occasions* (Chicago: Northwestern Press, 1998) notably promote the contemporary poetry avant-garde. The previously mentioned online Emily Dickinson archive (https://www.edickinson.org/) offers images of Dickinson's handwritten manuscripts and poems from various published editions.

Both Auden and Eliot enjoy easily available selected poetry editions: namely, W. H. Auden, *Selected Poems*, ed. Edward Mendelson (New York: Vintage International, 2007); and T. S. Eliot, *Selected Poems* (New York: Harcourt, 1962). Readers who want more of Auden might enjoy his *Collected Poems*, ed. Edward Mendelson (New York: Vintage, 1991). Both Auden and Eliot were brilliant critics. Auden's *The Dyer's Hand and Other Essays* (New York: Random House, 1988) and Eliot's *On Poetry and Poets* (New York: Farrar, Straus and Giroux, 1957) are good places to start. The two-volume scholarly edition, *The Poems of T. S. Eliot*, ed. Christopher Ricks and Jim McCue (Baltimore: Johns Hopkins University Press, 2015), offers invaluable information about the poems and the poet.

Index

American Poetry

Index

RELIGION
IN AMERICA
A Very Short Introduction
Timothy Beal

Timothy Beal describes many aspects of religion in contemporary America that are typically ignored in other books on the subject, including religion in popular culture and counter-cultural groups; the growing phenomenon of "hybrid" religious identities, both individual and collective; the expanding numbers of new religious movements, or NRMs, in America; and interesting examples of "outsider religion." He also offers an engaging overview of the history of religion in America, from Native American traditions to the present day. Finally, Beal highlights the three major forces shaping the present and future of religion in America.

www.oup.com/vsi

THE BLUES
A Very Short Introduction
Elijah Wald

This VSI provides a brief history of the blues genre's main movements and most influential artists and gives a sense of the breadth of the blues field. Beginning with the music's roots in African and African-American styles, European folk music, and popular forms such as minstrelsy and ragtime, it traces how blues evolved over the course of the twentieth century as both a discrete genre and a basic ingredient in virtually all American pop styles from jazz to hip-hop.

Genius
A Very Short Introduction
Andrew Robinson

Genius is highly individual and unique, of course, yet it shares
a compelling, inevitable quality for professionals and the general
public alike. Darwin's ideas are still required reading for every
working biologist; they continue to generate fresh thinking
and experiments around the world. So do Einstein's theories
among physicists. Shakespeare's plays and Mozart's melodies
and harmonies continue to move people in languages and
cultures far removed from their native England and Austria.
Contemporary 'geniuses' may come and go, but the idea of
genius will not let go of us. Genius is the name we give to a quality
of work that transcends fashion, celebrity, fame, and reputation:
the opposite of a period piece. Somehow, genius abolishes
both the time and the place of its origin.

www.oup.com/vsi

Racism
A Very Short Introduction
Ali Rattansi

From subtle discrimination in everyday life and scandals in politics, to incidents like lynchings in the American South, cultural imperialism, and 'ethnic cleansing', racism exists in many different forms, in almost every facet of society. But what actually is race? How has racism come to be so firmly established? Why do so few people actually admit to being racist? How are race, ethnicity, and xenophobia related? This book reincorporates the latest research to demystify the subject of racism and explore its history, science, and culture. It sheds light not only on how racism has evolved since its earliest beginnings, but will also explore the numerous embodiments of racism, highlighting the paradox of its survival, despite the scientific discrediting of the notion of 'race' with the latest advances in genetics.

www.oup.com/vsi

PROGRESSIVISM
A Very Short Introduction
Walter Nugent

This very timely *Very Short Introduction* offers an engaging overview of progressivism in America--its origins, guiding principles, major leaders and major accomplishments.

A many-sided reform movement that lasted from the late 1890s until the early 1920s, progressivism emerged as a response to the excesses of the Gilded Age, an era that plunged working Americans into poverty while a new class of ostentatious millionaires built huge mansions and flaunted their wealth. Progressives fought for worker's compensation, child labour laws, minimum wage and maximum hours legislation; they enacted anti-trust laws, instituted the graduated income tax, won women the right to vote, and laid the groundwork for Roosevelt's New Deal.

www.oup.com/vsi

ROMANTICISM
A Very Short Introduction
Michael Ferber

What is Romanticism? In this *Very Short Introduction*
Michael Ferber answers this by considering who the romantics
were and looks at what they had in common – their ideas, beliefs,
commitments, and tastes. He looks at the birth and growth
of Romanticism throughout Europe and the Americas, and
examines various types of Romantic literature, music, painting,
religion, and philosophy. Focusing on topics, Ferber looks at the
rising prestige of the poet; Romanticism as a religious trend;
Romantic philosophy and science; Romantic responses to the
French Revolution; and the condition of women. Using examples
and quotations he presents a clear insight into this very diverse
movement.

www.oup.com/vsi

FREE SPEECH
A Very Short Introduction
Nigel Warburton

'I disapprove of what you say, but I will defend to the death your right to say it' This slogan, attributed to Voltaire, is frequently quoted by defenders of free speech. Yet it is rare to find anyone prepared to defend all expression in every circumstance, especially if the views expressed incite violence. So where do the limits lie? What is the real value of free speech? Here, Nigel Warburton offers a concise guide to important questions facing modern society about the value and limits of free speech: Where should a civilized society draw the line? Should we be free to offend other people's religion? Are there good grounds for censoring pornography? Has the Internet changed everything? This Very Short Introduction is a thought-provoking, accessible, and up-to-date examination of the liberal assumption that free speech is worth preserving at any cost.

> 'The genius of Nigel Warburton's *Free Speech* lies not only in its extraordinary clarity and incisiveness. Just as important is the way Warburton addresses freedom of speech - and attempts to stifle it - as an issue for the 21st century. More than ever, we need this book.'
>
> Denis Dutton, University of Canterbury, New Zealand

www.oup.com/vsi